WE ARE
HERE TO STAY

WE ARE HERE TO STAY

VOICES OF UNDOCUMENTED YOUNG ADULTS

written and photographed by
SUSAN KUKLIN

CANDLEWICK PRESS

For Sarah, Meyer, Leah, Chaim,
for those who are here,
for those who will come.

First edition 2019

Library of Congress Catalog Card Number 2018960308
ISBN 978-0-7636-7884-5

18 19 20 21 22 23 VRP 10 9 8 7 6 5 4 3 2 1

Printed in East Peoria, IL, U.S.A.

This book was typeset in Mate and Avenir Next.

Candlewick Press
99 Dover Street
Somerville, Massachusetts 02144

visit us at www.candlewick.com

The book you are holding was scheduled to be published in 2017 with full-color portraits of the young people who were interviewed for it. Since that time, executive action regarding DACA recipients has been in flux, making it risky for many of the participants to reveal their identities. Their images, names, and other identifiers have been withheld to protect the inspiring people who share their stories in these pages.

CONTENTS

PART TWO: TWISTS AND TURNS

NOTES AND RESOURCES

TO THE READER

The nine young people featured in *We Are Here to Stay* could be your neighbors, classmates, friends, or even family members. For much of their lives, they've lived with a secret: they did not have any of the documents — U.S. passports, green cards, or visas — that identify them as legal residents or citizens of the United States. Without this documentation, they could be taken from their homes at any time and deported to the country of their birth. Beyond this constant threat of deportation to a place they may have barely remembered, if at all, they also did not have Social Security numbers, which would have authorized them to work. They were not eligible for health insurance or federal aid for college tuition. Other people often labeled them as illegals, aliens, criminals, and worse. Some described themselves as living in the shadows.

Many young undocumented people have come out of the shadows to disclose their status. No longer would they allow others to define who they are. This book is about these people. It is not about politics. And yet politics has come to play a significant role in many immigrants' lives. One crucial government program that is talked about throughout the book is the Deferred Action for Childhood Arrivals (DACA).

DACA was a two-year program, subject to renewal, that allowed temporary relief from deportation to undocumented persons between the ages of fifteen and thirty-one who came to the United States on or before June 15, 2007, and lived in the United States continuously for at least five years. It enabled them to have a Social Security number so that they could work. This program was not a path to citizenship.

It was an executive action, not a law in the traditional sense. The courts, Congress, or the president could withdraw DACA.

In September 2017, the president repealed DACA. Approximately 700,000 youths — attending school, working, or in the military — no longer knew what their future held. *We Are Here to Stay* was well on its way to publication at that time. We decided to stop the presses. Everyone in the book was disappointed; they wanted their story told. They did not want to go back into the shadows. In time, and after much deliberation, we all agreed that the young immigrants' experiences must be told. But to protect them, we disclose only their names' first initial, followed by a dash. Photographs and other identifiers have been removed.

It is my dream that the stories of the nine young people in *We Are Here to Stay* will encourage and facilitate an informed, reasonable, and honest conversation about the complexities of immigration. It is also my hope that we can one day republish this book with the participants' names, places, and photographs fully intact.

Susan Kuklin

PART ONE

COMING TO AMERICA

Portraits: Twins S— and D— with their sister Y—

CHAPTER ONE

LA FAMILIA, PART I
S——, D——, and Y——

Y—— and her younger siblings, twins S—— and D——, were born in Medellín, Colombia. They came to New York one by one when they were very young. Y—— says, "One of the reasons for leaving Colombia was our education. It was unclear if we stayed in Colombia that we could go to college. Another reason was my dad's entrepreneurial spirit. He saw the U.S. as an opportunity to have a better life. Also, there was more and more violence in Medellín, and our neighborhood was becoming unstable. There were turf wars." The children spoke no English. They had no idea what life would be like in a new country far from their tight extended family and friends. But they were together; they are a family.

So Far Away

S——: I remember *every* single detail from that day. My brother and I were Rollerblading outside. I was wearing my new sweat suit that my mother had sent the day before. I loved it so much. It had a cute Barbie on it. I remember being in the hospital and looking at the pants with a big hole and blood all over them. I thought, I hope someone can fix that.

There was a big sidewalk outside my house —

D——: The sidewalk was small. All my life I thought it was huge too, and then I looked at the pictures on Google Maps. It was this tiny little thing.

S——: I remember it as big.

Y——: You guys were only six, so little that everything seemed big back then.

S——: When we were Rollerblading, I heard gunshots, and I jumped off the sidewalk. I fell down and felt something hard on my left leg.

D——: Your right leg!

S——: Left! My left leg started hurting a lot. There was so much commotion. People were calling me to come to them. I was able to get up and Rollerblade about ten feet on one leg until I got to a little yard that led to our house. I got there and saw blood on the ground. I thought, what's going on? I never realized I had been shot.

D——: It was our babysitter's friend who saw the blood. Everybody thought S—— was limping because she fell on the Rollerblade. The friend started yelling, "She's dripping blood! She's dripping blood!" Our grandma turned and saw the blood. She picked S—— up and took her to a bus.

S——: Everyone on the bus got off right away so I could go to the hospital with my grandmother. Grandma was hysterical. She hoisted me up and passed me into the arms of our neighbor to help take me to the hospital.

Meanwhile, I'm thinking, please tell me this isn't happening. There was a priest who stayed on the bus. It was the weirdest thing. He did a prayer with us. I didn't understand why he was doing that.

My grandmother held my leg tight to help stop the blood. When we got to the hospital, there was even more chaos. People were looking at me, staring. Right. At. Me.

I do not remember the pain that much. I like to think I was a trouper through the whole thing. I remember not being scared, and I never lost consciousness. After surgery it hurt where they took out the bullet.

When my grandma came into the room to see me, I said, "Grandma, why didn't you fix yourself up before you brought me here?" She had blood on her arms and clothing, and her hair looked a mess. She couldn't believe I said that.

The wound wasn't serious, thank God. This kind of thing happened a lot in our neighborhood. It was more frightening for my parents. I was there, in Medellín, Colombia, and knew I was fine. But my mom and dad were here, in New York. On the phone they were asking things like, "Is she going to walk again?" My dad had gone to the diner where my mom worked to tell her about me. I could hear him saying, "She's fine. She's fine. S— got shot, but she's fine."

When my mother got on the phone, I was totally calm. "Mom, I'm fine." I wasn't even crying.

Y—: If I had had a gunshot wound, I would have been so dramatic. I'd have said, "Mommmmm, come back right now!"

S—: Y— and D— listen to my story over and over, as if I was telling it the first time.

D—: I saw when they killed the dude. I was right there. I was like, "Whoa, did that guy just get shot?" And then I saw my grandmother pick up S— and take her to the bus. I screamed, "WHAT'S GOING ON?" The neighbors told me she had been shot. I went to the hospital, but they wouldn't let me in because I was a little kid. S— was in surgery, and I was like, "Why aren't you letting me see my sister? I WANT TO SEE MY SISTER!"

I didn't see S—— for a week. I had to wait until she came home. I knew that she was going to be okay, but a whole week! Once S—— got home, everybody was giving her all the attention and all the presents. And I was jealous.

S——: You were jealous too, Y——.

Y——: I wasn't jealous.

D——: Everybody was jealous! There was, like, a line outside the house to visit her just because she got shot. One day I was playing PlayStation with my cousin in my grandma's apartment on the first floor. My uncle came and just shut the thing off. He said, "S—— wants the PlayStation." And he took it to the other room.

Y——: WHOA!

S—— laughs.

D——: So she's sitting there in the bed, and everybody's giving her gifts, and I'm thinking, okay, I should have gotten shot, maybe.

Y——: WHAAAAAAAAAAT?

When S—— got out, she couldn't walk very well. She had to do exercises for a whole year so that she wouldn't walk with a limp. It was hard for my parents, because that's the worst thing that could ever happen when they were so far away. Our mom wanted to come back, but that meant giving up all the resources they had put into establishing a life in New York. A thing like this was a reason why they went to America in the first place. It got my parents to work even harder.

We wanted to immigrate to the U.S., like other members of our family. But the law had changed. We went to the consulate in Bogotá and tried to get tourist visas. We were denied. If you are poor, they don't want you to visit, because they know you're going to stay. There were no legal paths for poor people to come to the States. There was a line for highly skilled laborers and a line for highly educated professionals. But we didn't fit those profiles. For example, I think the wait list for people from Mexico and the Philippines to come here is like twenty or twenty-five years — something ridiculous. It became impossible for poor people to immigrate through legal channels.

In Medellín

Y——: We lived in a really nice community, surrounded by cousins, our grandparents, and other family members. We lived in a house on top of a house on top of a house. Our maternal grandparents lived on the first floor, our aunt and uncle lived on the second floor with their kids, and we lived on the third floor.

Our father had grown up in a commune in Medellín, in one of the poorest, most marginalized neighborhoods in the city. When he was a little boy, he would sell ice cream in the neighborhood. In his late teens and early twenties, he drove a taxi, and he dressed up like Santa Claus in ninety-degree weather to take pictures with tourists.

By the time he emigrated, he owned a grocery store three blocks from our house. It was called *La Familia,* which is "The Family" in Spanish. The store did okay, but a business like that in Colombia is not enough to make ends meet for a family of five.

S——: Dad only went to school up to the fifth grade, but Mom stayed in school until the end of high school. She started working as a secretary. Pretty soon she met my dad.

D——: Dad was the poorest guy on the block.

S——: And Mom was the prettiest girl on the block.

Y——: After they married, Mom worked with Dad in *La Familia* until I was born. Although she still helped out at the store, she mostly stayed home and took care of me.

Our dad emigrated first. He had several family members and friends already living here who are documented. Then Mom came here a year later. She worked as a waitress in a diner. Her English was pretty bad. She learned how to say *bagel* and *bacon* before she learned basic English.

When our parents left, we stayed with our grandmother. Our aunt took care of us too. Although we had our cousins and family around us all the time, it sucked being away from our parents. That was terrible. The separation took a toll on all of us.

Before our parents left, we spent a lot of time together. Sunday was our family day, and we would go to the water park or do something else fun. I was very close to our mom, and I would tell her things, like what was happening at school. So when she left, and our dad had already been gone for a year, I felt kind of empty. I cried a lot.

S——: A young woman from the neighborhood was paid to take care of us so that our grandmother and aunt wouldn't have to do it all the time. I liked her.

Y——: I thought that my brother and sister were getting way too attached to this nanny. I worried that they were forgetting about our mom. Even though she was super nice, I was very mean to her. I was super jealous that she was taking my mom's place.

Mostly I was rude to her. Whenever she tried to discipline me, I'd yell, "You're not my mom! Who are you?" My mom would call me on the phone and tell me not to be so rude. But I was mad.

S——: Our parents found ways to keep in touch with us. They'd send us gifts during Christmas. They sent awesome toys and clothes and things . . .

D——: But that didn't make up for them not being there during Christmas. We made home videos for them all the time.

Y——: I made a video of my first Communion for my dad. I told him that I missed him and that I loved him.

New York

Y—, S—, and D— do not talk about how they came here;
they talk about what happened once they arrived.

Y—: When I turned ten, I came to New York. It was sad to say good-bye to everyone. Who knew how long it would be before I saw them again? The hardest part was leaving my grandmother. But I was excited about seeing my parents. And I liked the idea of being fearless and coming all by myself. I was scared a little too. Something bad could happen. Something could go wrong and I wouldn't make it to New York. I did a lot of praying.

When I arrived, my dad picked me up. Seeing him after two years was a very cool moment. It was February, and there was a huge snowstorm. I had never seen snow. It was so pretty and *so* cold. I love my dad. He's the sweetest, most amazing dad, and I had missed him so much.

Mom was working overtime that night and did not come to meet me. She says that's not true, she was there. My dad doesn't remember her being there. I don't remember her being there. Apparently there are two stories.

In a weird way it was awkward being with them again. One or two years is a long time in the life of a young girl. Mom wanted to be super close to me. There was a bathtub in the apartment. A bathtub is unheard of in Colombia. We had a showerhead but not a bathtub. My mom bought bubbles and stuff for my first bath. I hadn't seen her in a year and I felt awkward and self-conscious being naked in front of her.

It was winter, so we wore jackets and hats and gloves. My mom was beautiful. She wore a gray tight-fitting hat, and her long black hair slipped out of it on the sides. My parents held hands and looked at each other a lot. They rode in the front seat of the car with me in the backseat. They laughed and made jokes. It was so nice seeing them close again.

Ever since my father came to the States, he sold clothing out of a suit-case on the street. Our uncle had a small clothing store on the side of a CD shop. He gave our dad twenty pairs of jeans to start him off. Dad sold the jeans, made money, and bought more jeans from our uncle. Once I arrived, Dad and I sold clothes together after school. We'd go to hair salons and bakeries. Dad would ask the owner if he could sell clothes in the shop.

If they said no, he wouldn't go in, but he built really great relationships with those who said yes.

Our dad became well known in the neighborhood. I remember everyone being super happy when they met me, because they all knew Dad's story. They knew that he was working hard to bring his kids here. I was here, my mom was here, and my brother and sister were on their way. It was beautiful.

One day we did really well. But when we were driving out of the parking lot, I forgot to put on my seat belt. A policewoman stopped us and gave us a huge ticket. I was a minor and didn't have my seat belt on. We begged the officer not to do anything more. It was sad because we had done so well and then this huge ticket took all our profit away. And it was my fault!

Eventually Dad opened his own shop on the side of a hair salon. There was maybe one mannequin and some things on display. I think he was still selling clothes on the street to make extra money. The store was doing well. He bought another store with a business partner. Our dad's good at what he does. Eventually he had five stores, but we sold two last year.

D——: I came here a year after Y——, but I waited six months for S—— to arrive before I started school. My parents wanted us to be in the same grade, so I stayed home and played PlayStation One. I didn't have PlayStation Two yet.

Once S—— came to New York, we went to school. I felt like she was my boss. She would tell me, "Don't do this. Don't talk to that kid."

S——: When D—— and I lived in Colombia, we had a very good relationship, but when we came here, there was a big change. I'm not sure why. Maybe it was because I was still very attached to Colombia and I didn't want to leave. I would still love to go back. Every day of my life I think about going back. I have a lot of memories, like small details and stuff. The neighborhood, the church, my dad's parents' house, which was down the block, and a park called *La Estrella*.

D——: S——, do you remember the first day at school?

D— leans back in his chair, laughing.

S—: All I remember is the lunchroom incident. We laugh about it now but back then it wasn't so funny.

D—: We went down to lunch, right? But we didn't know where we were going. We ended up in the cafeteria, and we had left our lunch boxes upstairs. We didn't know what the word *lunch* meant. I started crying. And a teacher came and asked what's wrong in Spanish. And I'm, like, *"Dejamos la lonchera en el salón y tenemos hambre."* ["We left the lunch box in the classroom, and I'm hungry."]

S—: We didn't speak English at all . . .

D—: And we were embarrassed.

S—: At first I thought D— was never going to learn English.

D—: But I'm pretty good now. At this point we don't speak Spanish to each other. We speak Spanish to our parents. Even with my parents there, I address Y— and S— in English. And I don't know when that began. Y— says that some of the things we say to each other would be rude in Spanish, things like "Shut up!" In Spanish that would sound nasty.

Undocumented

S—: We always knew that we were undocumented. We knew we were here illegally. There was never any question about that. Lots of people in our community were undocumented, so we didn't feel different. But we knew it wasn't a good thing. We knew that we shouldn't feel too comfortable revealing it. Kids in my high school were mostly documented. They'd say, "Wow, you don't have a Social? You don't have a driver's license? What are you going to do?"

D——: When I was younger and living here, I thought, maybe if I tell anybody I'm undocumented, I'll get arrested. So I was careful. Other than that, transitioning here wasn't too hard for me. It was kind of exciting.

S——: Not for me. It was not easy being here, because I was angry all the time. I was angry that I had to leave all my friends and my family in Medellín. I didn't want to be here. I missed our house. I missed our neighborhood. I missed being happy. I guess I took it out on D——.

D——: Uh-huh!

S——: D—— started making friends immediately. I only wanted to be with our family.

D——: I feel like I used to have a lot of loser friends. A lot of the friends that I had back in the day were not like — I'm not saying they are bad kids; they were just not motivated. They didn't go to school. They just wanted to get by. And I'm not like that. I want to go to school. You know how a lot of kids nowadays are like, "Oh, I want to be cool." You know? And they'd flash money. I'm not that kind of kid. I'm like, "Hey, what's up? Can you lift a hundred-pound dumbbell?" I'm into working out. So if you don't work out, you're not my friend.

When I was ten, eleven, twelve, I started telling people I was undocumented. I felt comfortable telling all of my good friends. They said, "What does that mean?"

"I can't leave the country."

And they said, "Oh, okay."

As we grew up, there was more pressure on us. My dad said, "You always have to do the right thing — remember, you are not like them." For example, when my dad saw me around kids who smoked weed, he'd say, "Don't get into that stuff. You know you're undocumented. You get caught, you're out! If the others get caught, they'd get a fine or something. For you it's a completely different story." It was his way to keep me from doing anything bad.

I guess people like us have to work harder. I have this friend; he's undocumented too. He didn't graduate high school. He just hangs out with all these kids who spend the day smoking weed or drinking and doing all these crazy things. I tried to talk to him because he was a close friend of mine. "Dude, I don't want to be mean or anything, but eventually you guys are going to be broke, and one of you will come up with the idea of selling weed or something. Once you get caught up in that game, you'll be arrested, and you're out of here."

He works construction, so he makes money. I tell him, "Do you want to do that for the rest of your life? Like, really? Really?" He doesn't have ambition. If you don't have papers, I feel that you should be more ambitious than anybody else.

Y——: Can I say something about that? Sure, it's true that undocumented people have to work hard because of their circumstances and stuff, but at the end of the day, undocumented people are no different from others, aside from their papers. I don't think the story about your friend says anything about undocumented immigrants as much as it does about kids growing up under particular circumstances.

D——: Yeah, that's true. We're like any other family, trying to make the best of it. I did cut school sometimes, but that doesn't have anything to do with being undocumented. I would walk to school with S—— and say, "Hey, S——, would you tell Mommy I was in school?" She would get really mad, but I knew she wouldn't tell. She wouldn't do that to me. Right, S——? Right?

S——: I don't hear you, D——. I was always a good kid in school. I always did my homework. I studied a lot. I didn't have any distractions, because I didn't hang out at all. There are two things I'm passionate about: music and politics. I decided to be a politics major in college because I'm interested in social justice and immigration rights.

During my senior year in high school, there was this program called We the People. It was a series of mock congressional hearings. We worked in groups. I wrote all our group's essays discussing the Universal Declaration of Human Rights. I loved writing the papers. I guess that's what got me into such a good college.

I didn't want to go away to college, but my sister visited the college once and gave it a great review. Because I'm undocumented, they consider me an international student. I got some loans, but the tuition is much higher for international students than it is for U.S. citizens. At least I'm not paying in full.

My brother chose a school near home.

D——: I got into my college, and we received the bill. It was a lot. They were charging me as an out-of-state student, which was five thousand dollars a semester. And we were like, nah, nah, nah, this was supposed to be, like, three thousand dollars. I had signed an affidavit that basically said that I was going to fix my immigration status. It's like a promise. Once I fix my immigration status, my tuition goes way down.

When Deferred Action for Childhood Arrivals (DACA) was put in place, D—— and his sisters signed up. In New York State, DACA holders pay the same rate as residents.

Now I pay what everyone who is a state resident pays. But because I'm undocumented, I'm not eligible for government financial aid. When I'm in school and somebody brings up financial aid, I go, "Oh, I don't have financial aid."

"Why? Your parents make too much money?"

And I'm like, "Yeah. That's why." I don't say I'm undocumented here in college. Never.

DACA couldn't have come at a better time. By my senior year in high school, I was a really good athlete. One of the coaches said, "You should try out for lifeguarding. You can make five thousand dollars for the summer." I thought, wow, five thousand dollars! I practiced hard. To become a lifeguard you had to do two laps in thirty-five seconds. When I tried out for the job, I did the two laps in 34.8 seconds. I was, like, YES!

At the pool where I tried out, everyone had to fill out an application. It asked for my Social Security number, and I didn't know what to do. I called my mom.

"Mom, what'll I do?"

"I don't know."

"Should I put in a fake number or something like that?" Well, Mom wasn't too keen on my doing that. Then I saw another kid's application. The Social Security was left blank. "Should we just leave it like that?" I asked him.

"Yeah, yeah, just leave it." I gave in the application and said I would return later with a work permit number. I was, like, praying that DACA would come through before the application deadline. I was lucky because our DACA cards came two days before the deadline.

My dad reminds us every day that we are lucky to have DACA. "You don't want to lose this. You'll lose your car. You'll lose your job." He doesn't have to say this, because I've become pretty serious. I don't have time for a lot of things. I work, go to school, and then the gym. That's my life. I live in Queens, and I go to school in Brooklyn. So let's say I go up to a nice girl and say, "Hey, where do you live?"

"I live in Ridgewood."

Oh, damn, that's so far. "Never mind." And I stay by myself. This semester I changed my schedule so I'm only in school two days a week. I don't get to see many people. I'm not saying I don't have any friends. I have a few friends, but it's not like, "Hey, what's up, best friend? When are we going to a movie?"

S——: My freshman year of college was not what I expected. There was so much drama. I was very chill. I was always by myself. I needed my family. I stayed in my room for most of the first year. My sister, Y——, was the one person I called. She'd call me too, to see that I was okay.

D——: I think that what made us the way we are is the struggle we saw our parents go through. It's like they work so hard for us, how can we fail? We have to succeed.

Y——: I kind of have that philosophy too. We're blessed with great parents who did so much for us. The more blessings you have, the more you have to give back. The harder it is, the more you try. And then the blessings accumulate. I want to do so much more because I'm getting so much more.

S——: Before college, my mom talked to me about the way I treat D——. I knew I was being mean. I knew I made him feel bad and I backed away a little bit. Then, when I went away to college, I really missed him. We're best friends now. I think we have a good relationship.

D——: Yep.

S——: And my sister is very protective of me.

Y——: You think I'm protective?

S——: Yes. You look after me. I think you do.

Y——: Awwww. That's so nice. I guess I kind of do.

D——: Y—— became really smart. I think we've all grown in the last years.

S——: During my sophomore year, I saw an older girl putting up a poster that read, "If you are undocumented, come to this meeting." I thought, okay. Five of us who were undocumented came. I loved being there. It was such a safe space. When we shared our experiences, it felt really good.

Now I campaign at college to bring about awareness of the undocumented student experience. Recently we held a dialogue with other students. Over thirty-five people showed up, and we shared our stories about coming to America.

D——: Some people make it seem so easy to get papers. Yesterday, my cousin said to me, "You should get married. Then you'll get to be a citizen." No, it doesn't work that way.

"We're best friends now."

Y——: It's insulting for me to hear that, because I've been fighting for the DREAM Act immigration legislation for a long time.

> *The DREAM Act was a legislative proposal to grant immigrants conditional residency and, upon meeting further qualifications, permanent residency. Y—— explains what happened to it in the next chapter.*

Why should I have to marry someone to be a citizen? What if I don't want to marry a U.S. citizen?

S——: What if I don't want to marry at all?

Y——: YES! YES!

S——: There's something I need to say. When many of those involved in the undocumented youth movement refer to having an American identity, we don't mean that we like apple pie, watch baseball, or celebrate certain holidays in the same way that traditional white American families do. We mean that by coming here at a young age, and by receiving a K-through-twelve education, we've learned to navigate a web of institutions or systems that are not designed to include or consider undocumented immigrants. We learned to do this all on our own. K-through-twelve schooling is important because it functions as an assimilation engine.

Our integration is a very different experience from that of our parents, who only had the opportunity to work and not to go to school. My siblings and I speak English fluently. We've gone to school here almost our whole lives. But that doesn't mean that we've obtained an American identity. I think what I'm trying to say is that we've obtained a *marginalized* American identity because identity is so tied to race, language, and culture. It is a marginalized American identity that is not remorseful. It does not abandon my Latinidad or "Colombian-ness," which is incredibly central to whom I am.

Nevertheless, being undocumented doesn't define me. I don't want documents or, for that matter, the fact that I got shot to be my signifier.

Ultimately, I'm just a person. If I were in a room where I had to introduce myself, I would say I'm a person who loves music and politics.

S—, D—, and Y— do not take their family and their academic good fortunes for granted. They are currently working to make a difference and give back to their community.

Portrait: Y—

CHAPTER TWO

LA FAMILIA, PART II
Y——

*Like many older siblings, Y—— paved the way for S——
and D——. She was the first of the children to come to
the United States. She was the first to learn English. She
was the first to go to college. And she was the first to
participate as an activist for undocumented immigrants.
Y——'s story begins at a college panel for the parents of
incoming freshmen.*

Recently I was on a panel for the incoming freshmen's parents. I was asked to share my experiences as a university student. I told the parents that I was part of the university's DREAM Team [a campus group that seeks to further understanding about undocumented immigrants]. I told them that activism was important to me because I'm undocumented.

Everyone was silent as I spoke. Should I have shared that? But I did it because it's an opportunity to pull in allies. Maybe next time they hear someone railing about how terrible immigrants are, they'll think about me. I'm a real person. I go to school with their kids. I have a wonderful family. Maybe after listening to me they will feel differently about immigrants.

Afterwards, one of the parents came up to me and said, "Thank you so much for sharing that information. I'm so sorry our country hasn't done something to change your status. It's really embarrassing. I hope we can change things soon."

When I have moments like that, it reaffirms my commitment to help bring about change. Telling people who I am is a super-liberating experience.

A lot of people grow up with shame and anxiety about being undocumented. It's not something you want to share with people. On the news you hear about "the illegals," and about all the resources they take from Americans. I don't think people have a particularly nice image of us. So when I say, "I'm undocumented," it's hard to tell how people are going to react.

When I was in high school, I shared my story publicly, and then my best friend shared her story. Then another person stepped forward and shared her story. Although there were common threads, we all had different experiences. What we have in common is that we want to be United States citizens. We want to be an accepted part of society. Why don't you allow us to be part of society? We want to contribute. I wanted to become a teacher. Now I want to become a professor.

I got a lot of lucky breaks here and feel really blessed. When I left Medellín, Colombia, I never thought I would end up in a great university. There's no reason why I should have ended up in a college like this other than my studying.

My parents also feel lucky. They are so proud of their children. Many immigrant families have such a hard time. My dad can pay part of the tuition, and I can pay part of the tuition. My sister is getting a great education. And my brother is also working toward a degree in business. Our parents had a huge role in all of this.

Schoolgirl in America

In Colombia, I had skipped a year. But when I came here, I was put back in fourth grade for the first six months because of my age. They didn't put me in the bilingual ESL classes. The principal told my mom to let me finish fourth grade in a regular English class because then I'd be immersed in the language and I'd learn faster. I was in class for eight hours and didn't understand anything.

In elementary school the struggle was not that I was undocumented; it was that I couldn't speak English. Although everyone in class was either black or Latino, I was still the odd one out because I couldn't speak English. They teased me.

Every day I'd come home and say, "Mom, I don't want to be here. Send me back to Colombia. I hate this place. I hate everyone." There was a lot of bullying. I knew they were making fun of me, but I didn't understand what they were saying. One time in the cafeteria, a girl made me stand up, and she said, "Ugly." The others were laughing about me. I recognized the word *ugly* because of *Shrek*. I knew they were saying something mean about me.

Also my clothes. We didn't have a lot of extra money. I wore the same pair of sneakers and the same sweater the whole year. Kids are really into fashion, I guess, and clothes are a marker of your status.

How did Y— win over the kids?

I don't think I did. There were two girls who became friends with me because both were Colombian. But they were super mean to me too. One would hit me or punch me or throw random things at me. They used to buy gummy bears near the corner of my school, and during lunchtime they would literally hand out the gummy bears to everyone but me. And we sat together!

One time, when I was in high school, I went to that store and bought gummy bears just for myself. I guess I was reminiscing about those times.

I think I learned English fast because of the bullying and stuff, and feeling so terrible. In Colombia, education was really, really important to me. I went as far as fifth grade in Colombia and I was used to being the top student. Then suddenly I came here, and the only thing I understood was math class. I understood math because it was numbers. I'd see equations on the board, and I'd say to myself, okay, I know what that is.

At home, my mom and I would literally sit for hours translating words, trying to figure out what it was the teacher wanted me to do. My mom took out a Spanish–English dictionary, and we'd go word for word, figuring it out. We struggled through that together. I'm so grateful for my mom. She'd come home from work super tired but still made time for me because she wanted me to do well.

My fifth-grade teacher was a Cuban woman. For some reason she liked me, and I really liked her. I grew close to her, and she helped me with the language. By sixth grade I didn't have any issues with English. I spoke perfectly.

I still had issues with the other students, though. The class issue, the sneaker issue — which is what I called it — was still a problem. The kids were still pretty mean. But I did make one or two friends.

Middle School

My middle school was one of the worst in Queens. People were rowdy. Teachers were totally disrespected. One friend would straight-up not go to school. She would pick me up in the mornings and we'd walk to the corner, and I'd go to school and she'd go to a party.

One time in eighth grade, I cut school to go to one of these parties. I always went to school, but the party was happening at my best friend's house, and I wanted to be there. When her mom found out, the party was broken up, and my friend got into big trouble. Then my friend's mom went straight to our clothing store, where Mom was now working, and told her that I was there too. My parents were devastated.

My mom was really offended. She was angry. She took my phone away. When my dad came home, he took me into a little room. He didn't scream at me; he just started crying. "Is this what we brought you here for?" he said.

This is a thing about immigrant kids. When their parents pull out that story — *Is this what we brought you here for?* — it's more hurtful than anything. I remembered Colombia and what our struggles were like. I saw how hard my parents worked to bring us here. My dad crying is still fresh in my mind. Oh, my God, I'm a terrible daughter.

I need to figure out how to phrase this: there are a lot of wrong turns immigrant kids can take because of the neighborhoods they come to and the problems they are thrown into that have nothing to do with their parents. To our parents, it seems like, you're here, there are so many opportunities for you now, go out and get them.

I think a lot of parents are disappointed when their kids don't actually succeed in the States. But that's because there are so many other barriers to deal with — the bullying, the bad influences, the poverty, not knowing the language and customs. There are just so many things to take you down.

I definitely went all out to become a cool person in middle school. I definitely fought hard for cool sneakers. I definitely fought hard to feel like I belonged to the cool crowd. The cool crowd was not the does-very-well-in-school crowd. It was the we-cut-school-and-have-great-parties crowd. In hindsight, elementary school was all about learning English and trying to adapt, and middle school was about pushing to be as cool as possible, as American as possible.

In middle school I started having boyfriends. I never hid my boyfriends from my parents. My parents encouraged us to hang out at our house rather than someplace else. I guess we were different from other immigrant kids who had more traditional backgrounds. My mom is awesome because she's always had an open relationship with us about everything.

I still kept good grades in middle school. A lot of my friends were straight-up failing all their classes.

What changed for me was high school. I was able to go to a high school that was out of my district. It was a much better school. There are three good public high schools in Queens, and I went to one of them, just by luck.

I applied there because my cousin told me that a lot of Colombian kids went there. "Oh, cool." I never considered the fact that it was a good high school. It was because Colombian kids were there. But that school totally changed me. I wouldn't be at such a good university if it weren't for that school. No. I don't think so.

High-School Activista

All of a sudden, I was surrounded by kids who cared about school. I wanted to be like that too.

One time I went to the library and asked the librarian to recommend a book. She gave me *The Kite Runner*. I loved it. That book changed everything for me. Suddenly the world was bigger than my family and me; it was bigger than Queens and Colombia. I connected to people on the other side of the world in our common vulnerability to suffering. It opened up historical, geographical, and political perspectives and sparked my social consciousness in a deep way. I kept going to the library every week, and I've been reading ever since.

I also started to become super public about my status. In the summer of my sophomore year, I heard about a conference for undocumented Latino youth given at the New York State Youth Leadership Council [also referred to as YLC]. There was a workshop there called Coming Out of the Shadows, which was modeled after the LGBTQ notion of coming out of the closet. They declared that we could not sit back and allow this impression of who an undocumented person is to be taken over by people who didn't know who we really are. We wanted to reclaim our identity.

The people there were awesome. I joined the organization and became an activist in the immigration movement.

Getting arrested was a huge worry. One of my friends, who is amazing, came out of the shadows in front of the ICE [Immigration and Customs Enforcement] building. It was crazy. No one knew what was going to happen. No one knew how people were going to react. No one knew if we'd all get arrested.

This was the first time I was with a large group of undocumented students. Hearing their issues, I realized that theirs were the same issues as mine. And then I learned there's this bill, the DREAM Act, which can help us become accepted members of society. I started caring about other people's undocumented issues, and I went with them to rallies in Washington multiple times.

Our senator, Charles Schumer, was on a committee that pushed bills forward in Congress. Although he was for the DREAM Act, he wasn't moving the bill. The activists from the YLC, who by now had become my friends, held a hunger strike right outside Senator Schumer's office. What amazing courage they had. They inspired me.

We began to share our immigration status publicly. We would get together in a super-public space, like Union Square in Manhattan, and chant,

Tell me what democracy looks like,
This is what democracy looks like . . .

Then each of us would take a microphone and share our stories with the people who gathered to hear us.

My parents worried about this. But they have always been supportive about everything that I did. And they believed in the cause.

The whole family was so, so supportive. They were proud of me, and proud of what we were doing. Every time they saw a rally on TV, they'd say, "Thank you for what you are doing." My aunts and uncles said, "Good for you! Share your story. Do it!"

During my junior year in high school, I connected with another program, which brings together minority students from across the country and works to get them into the college pipeline. I filled out the application, and my counselor sent it off. The organization was going to reject it unread based on my immigration status. It was one of the first instances where I felt discriminated against for not having papers. I was totally devastated. "WHY? Why am I different from other students? I have the same grades." I just wanted them to read my application. "Just read it! They're totally disqualifying me on the basis of my not having papers." My counselor advocated on my behalf. He called them back and got them to read my application. I got in.

Between my junior and senior year of high school, I went to a college-preparation program at an Ivy League university. I had never seen a place so beautiful. We drove up in the evening and the lamps were on. We walked to the dorm where I was to live. My parents were blown away.

I took courses in sociology, and had SAT prep twice a week. I'm grateful for this organization, obviously, because they are a huge reason why I'm here. Without them I wouldn't even have thought about an Ivy League school.

University

> *Like her siblings, Y— is considered an international student. She says, "The university gives a generous financial package to anyone who is eligible but can't afford tuition. The aid is the same for U.S. and international students, which is not true of other schools. Usually international students get much less private financial support."*

When undocumented students apply to schools, they know that they must pay ridiculous amounts of money to get in. It's frustrating knowing that close friends who are as qualified and as smart as I am and as dedicated as I am have to take so many semesters off because they need to save up to pay for school. Some of them have been in the States longer than I have. Some of them came here when they were just one year old, two years old. This is a huge barrier for undocumented students.

My Border Ethics class covers so many issues that relate to my life. Should we restrict immigration? Should we have more immigration?

"I went to a college-preparation program
at an Ivy League university."

Should we have open borders? It's been a good experience being in that class — especially seeing how thoughtful and receptive students are to others' struggles. They understand that immigration is not an easy issue. They think critically. Some students are not for immigration. We never get into arguments. I step back and detach myself because I want to hear what they have to say. But I also speak out from my own perspective. What would my life have become had I not come here? What does it mean for people like me in search of a better life?

DREAMer

DREAMer is the term for an undocumented youth who qualified for the DREAM Act.

In 2010, our group of DREAMers was working toward the passage of the DREAM Act, which was soon to be in front of Congress. Congress had been arguing this bill and finally it was coming to a vote. It passed the House, and it looked like it was going to pass the Senate. This was the most historic, exciting moment for us. The week before the vote, I went to a YLC meeting. One girl said, "I can feel it. I can feel it. It's definitely going to pass." She gave out such good vibes in the room. We were so excited.

I went to D.C. with busloads of about two hundred students, DREAMers, to watch the vote in the visitors' section of the Senate chamber. We were filled with hope and anticipation. DREAMers from all over the country gathered together. It was the first time many of us were meeting each other. There were so many people from so many different places and cultures, and yet we were all connected by the same situation. We ate together. We sang together. We hugged and we prayed. We made it clear that whatever happened, we would keep fighting.

The Senate chamber was really intimidating. We were up in the gallery looking down on the senators who were deciding our future, and yet we couldn't speak or intervene in any way. All we could do was hold our breath and one another's hands. Many of the students wore caps and gowns as a symbol of our aspirations, and in place of our voice, our bodies became the statement. The room was thick with tension. The bill had already passed in the House, and this was it. I felt the culmination of my work in the past year, and the work of others who had fought for this bill for over a decade.

As we sat through the debate, we heard some of the senators say all sorts of terrible things about us.

"These people are criminals."

"They are illegal."

It was so shocking to hear this. We could not defend ourselves. We had to be quiet. We were literally holding hands and crying in silence while those people were shoving our dreams out the door. We had fifty-five votes but we needed sixty to stop a filibuster.

The DREAM Act failed to pass. It was devastating.

After the vote, we were all crying. This was the closest we had come, and still it wasn't enough. When the DREAM Act didn't pass Congress, which is supposed to be the most representative body of America, it felt like a confirmation that the citizens don't want us here.

I wondered why I had to put up with this. Should I go to a place that really wants me? Should I go to a place where I don't have to hear "Deport them all!" "We hate you!" "Go back to where you came from!"

I thought about going back to Colombia after I graduated. Even though the United States is the country that has done amazing things for me, the country that gave me a great education, I can't function as a full citizen here. Why shouldn't I pursue opportunities elsewhere? The world is big. There are other places that would want to take me in. I've learned great skills and speak fluent English. I can get a good job somewhere.

But at the same time, I consider myself from Queens. I love my neighborhood so much. I would miss my friends. I would miss speaking English all the time. There are so many things about the United States that I don't want to leave. This is my home. It was a terrible time.

When the DREAM Act didn't pass, activists pushed President Barack Obama for some relief. Two years later, in 2012, he announced Deferred Action for Childhood Arrivals (DACA). At first many students didn't apply for Deferred Action. They were afraid that they would then be in the system and would be targeted.

I chose to sign up for DACA. I wasn't afraid of deportation, because I knew lawyers who told me it was okay. DACA enabled me to have a Social Security number, a work permit, and a driver's license. It's awesome. But I still couldn't vote. I still couldn't leave the country without something called advanced parole. My status is super discretionary. My brother and sister have Deferred Action too, but my parents are not eligible. This is only for students.

The reason we're here is that my parents wanted something better for their kids. The single, most important choice that they made in my eyes was deciding to give us a better life, and then putting all their energy into doing that. If it weren't for them, we wouldn't be here. And because of our parents' efforts, we feel we owe them. It would be really sad to get citizenship without our parents getting it. They made all the sacrifices; we've just come along for the ride and are receiving all the benefits.

My college friends and I started the university's DREAM Team. We talked with various senators in D.C., along with the YLC, about in-state tuition for undocumented students. The YLC helped change my life. I wonder how much more ashamed I would be about my status if I hadn't had workshops with them back in high school, how much more frustrated I would be if I hadn't been in a national movement to end deportation. Our group continues having regular meetings. We continue having phone-bank sessions where we call senators. We take buses to rallies in D.C. I hand out fliers here on campus.

I'm so thankful to be a part of something like that. And also, if I weren't part of the DREAM Team, I would not have met C—.

C——

C——, lean and lanky, with light brown hair and a Canadian passport, is also a student at the university. He met Y—— at the student center when Y—— was handing out a petition for the DREAM Act. What happened next? C—— looks to Y——, smiling. "You tell it."

Okay. I was petitioning the school to publicize the fact that they accept undocumented students. Or maybe it was a petition for the DREAM Act? I think it was a petition for the DREAM Act. I was gathering signatures for the petition. Whenever you talk to people about this, they say, "Okay, where can I sign?" Or "Okay, bye." But then C—— came, and he asked, "What is this? I never heard of this. I'm from Canada."

So I started talking about the DREAM Act and immigration, all the while thinking, he's so nice. I invited him to come to a movie screening about undocumented immigrants. And he came. I thought, wow, he actually came. That's so nice.

> *C——: I knew nothing about it, so I was interested. But that doesn't mean that she didn't seem like a very nice girl.*

Annnywaay, I asked him to come to Casino Night. It's this random thing that our college does. And he came to that too.

> *C——: There was this crazy face-painting station. I was there with about ten other guys from my dorm, and they were going, "Oh, look at all these people getting their faces painted. I would never get my face painted."*
>
> *Then Y—— came over and said, "Oh, you should have your face painted." I must have liked her, because I did it right away. The guys were laughing and shaking their heads at me. I had sparkles all over.*

"Maybe we should get dinner together?"

He asked me out on a date through Facebook. It was so cute. I don't know what he said exactly, but he was like, he was trying to be funny.

C—: *Trying?*

No, you really were funny. He said, "Oh, I think we had a great time," or something. Then he said something funny. And then he said, "Maybe we should get dinner together?" And I was like, "Okay." I was really excited because I never get dates like that. Usually guys would say, "Yo! Wanna go to the movies?" We've been together ever since.

Summer at the Border

I'm in a creative writing program. I write poetry. Because I wanted to write poetry about the collective struggle of immigrants, I wanted to see what the border looked like. I needed to see the border's physical space. I had to see it to feel it. I got a grant from the university to go to the border and write about immigration.

I was so close to the border, I could actually touch Mexico. I wondered what it felt like for people who came from Mexico. They were people just like I was ten years ago, twelve years ago. They were now going through the same struggle I went through. That sucked.

That summer, many unaccompanied minors were crossing the border. I'm talking about children who are eight, ten years old. And people were screaming at them, "Go home! We don't want you!" It was just so shameful. It made me angrier than when the DREAM Act hadn't passed. I could not understand how seeing kids, unaccompanied minors, didn't move people's hearts. I again asked myself, why am I here? Why is the world so terrible? Do I really want to be part of a country that doesn't care about unaccompanied minors? I know that's not all America is, and I know that that's not how all Americans feel, but when stuff like that happens, I get really frustrated.

Here's the flip side: I visited a bunch of shelters. There were many American citizens who were first responders to this crisis. So many generous people donated food and time to care for these children, even though they didn't have any connection with them, even though they didn't speak their language. They saw human beings in trouble and wanted to help. There were moms who were there day in and day out, volunteering. There were people who took time off from work because they felt that they were in the middle of a huge crisis. That was so awesome. It gave me hope.

In San Diego, I went right up to the fence. There was this student from New Jersey who also had Deferred Action. He was there to meet his mom, whom he hadn't seen in ten years. If you see the fence there, it has small holes and you can put your fingertips through. There's a section there where the guards let you stand. This guy had flown his mom all the way from Puebla to Tijuana. He had flown all the way from New Jersey to San Diego just so they could meet for a few hours and touch fingers. She didn't have papers to come here, and he didn't have advanced parole to leave. He was so close to her but they couldn't hug. I talked to him about it. He said, "A lot of people told me not to do it because of how terrible it felt to be so close and yet so far." But he said that he was glad he did it, just to hear her voice and see part of her face.

The first time I met a Border Patrol guard, I was scared. I was with a group of artists, actually, who do projects at the border. We were walking very close to the Rio Grande. But in order to touch the water, you have to go down a bank. A Border Patrol guy was there in his car, so one of the artists went up to him, and with a cute singsong voice said, "Oh, hi. We're with this student. She's from a college up North. She'd, like, she'd like to see the border."

"Oh, sure. Fine," he said, looking us over.

We went down to the river. I got to touch the water. Mexico was on the other side. Next to us were a bunch of footprints from people who had crossed the night before.

The guards wait until nighttime to catch people at that spot. This felt so awkward. Why am I allowed to be here and not them? It reminded me how privileged I am now because of Deferred Action. It reminded me how far I am from the experiences of someone who's trying to get into the country. But it also reminded me how connected I am to these immigrants because at one time I was one of them. And it reminded me once again how far away I feel from being a real, 100 percent U.S. citizen.

Spending time at the border region this summer made me appreciate New York City a lot more. I feel like I belong here. I don't feel people are out to get me. New York is a welcoming place. Coming out in Union Square is definitely not like coming out in Phoenix, Arizona.

Coming out in Phoenix or Tucson, Arizona? Whoa. There are so many reasons why I would be scared.

Nogales, Mexico, and Nogales, USA
Two towns, one name,
one fence.

CHAPTER THREE

NO MORE DEATHS
A PHOTO-ESSAY
Reverend John Fife

Tucson, Arizona
Early one morning

Like Y—, this author needed to see the border in order to write about it. The Reverend John Fife, who served as minister of the Southside Presbyterian Church in Tucson, Arizona, agreed to be my guide. John, as everyone calls him, is a legend in the human rights community. He is a member of the Sanctuary Movement—a volunteer group that provides safe haven for Central American refugees—and he is cofounder of No More Deaths [also known as No Más Muertes*]—a volunteer organization that provides water, food, and medical aid to undocumented immigrants crossing the Sonoran Desert by foot.*

Tall and thin, with sunburned skin and warm, penetrating eyes, John hugs or high-fives the folks at the church's soup kitchen who are cooking, serving, and eating breakfast. He checks out the front lawn, where groups of immigrants wait as pickup trucks stop by, offering jobs to day workers. The immigrant workers are self-organized on a first-come-first-served basis and according to work preference and salary. One church volunteer keeps a daily list. If the hourly wage being offered is not suitable, the workers need not accept it.

Traveling with us this day is my husband, Bailey, and Kathryn Ferguson, a writer, filmmaker, and Tucson Samaritans volunteer.

Before leaving, John takes out a map covered with red dots. "This is the Tucson side of the border. Each one of those red dots is where dead bodies were found."

"OH, MY GOD!" The mass of red spots on the map is shocking.

"We've been putting red dots on top of red dots. A wall was built in Nogales and across this valley. The result is that the wall pushed the migration into the most deadly areas: the mountains. The fence does not extend into the mountains. There are many trails in the mountains and desert. They are like spiderwebs. In the last twelve years, between 133 and 247 bodies have been found each year. And imagine, that's only the people who are found. It goes on and on."

To lower—no, to stop—the high number of deaths in the desert, John and his volunteers set up a No More Deaths campsite. We plan to visit the campsite, walk some of the trails, and see the border.

We climb into John's SUV, which is filled with cases of water, peanut-butter sandwiches, protein bars, and medical supplies. As we drive to the desert, John provides the following background information:

John: Historically, the border between Mexico and the United States was open. People traveled back and forth. In 1994, for the first time, the U.S. government said, "We're going to secure the border." They saw that most people migrated through a few Mexican border towns because they were the easiest and safest places to cross.

Matamoros to Brownsville, Texas
Nuevo Laredo to Laredo, Texas
Juárez to El Paso, Texas
Tijuana to San Diego, California
Nogales to Nogales, Arizona

The government's plan was really easy. They changed the eight-foot cyclone fence that marked the border in the cities to an eighteen-foot steel wall. They quadrupled the number of Border Patrol agents and vehicles and added technology, helicopters, and tracking dogs. This, they believed, would stop the migration.

Once that happened, the migrants tried to go around the fenced cities. Then the government said, "We're going to add even more Border Patrol agents and extend the fence to push the migrants far from those cities. People will still go around, but they will have to go through"— in their words —"the most hazardous areas of the border." We knew what that meant: roughly translated, "the deadliest areas."

Then they said, "We're going to ramp up the enforcement in Texas and California first, because no one will try to cross Arizona's Sonoran Desert. It's just too deadly."

The government succeeded in ramping up the enforcement and pushed much of the migration to the Sonoran Desert. And we've been the epicenter since then.

Who comes?

It used to just be guys coming to work. They saved some money and went home to their families. Then they'd come back when they needed more cash. A lot of the work was seasonal. It was a good deal for everybody. Then, when the militarization of the border started, those guys couldn't go back and forth anymore. It was too expensive and too hazardous. The migration was literally walled up. They stayed in the United States and saved their money to hire *coyotes* to bring their wives and kids here.

That's when we started seeing dead and dying children and women and men for the first time. It just breaks your heart.

How did you get involved in this movement?

I got mixed up with the Quakers. It's their fault. [*He says this with a smile.*] Back in the eighties, there was another crisis on the border. Immigrants were fleeing from civil wars in El Salvador and Guatemala. The United States refused to recognize them as refugees. They were deported and killed. So this Quaker friend came to me and said, "John, the United States won't recognize these people as refugees. Under the circumstances, I don't think we have any choice. We have to start smuggling them safely across the border."

And I said, "How the hell do you figure that?"

He pointed to history. "When the abolition folks smuggled runaway slaves across state lines to freedom, we got it right. Right?"

"Yeah. Right."

Then he pointed to the almost total failure to protect Jewish refugees fleeing the Nazis in the thirties and forties, and said, "We got it wrong then. Right?"

"Yeah."

"So we can't allow that to happen a second time, in our time, on our border, can we?"

How could I, a minister of God, a human being, turn my back on people who were dying? Sooooooo, there was a group of maybe twenty-two of us who started smuggling refugees from El Salvador and Guatemala across the border.

It took the Border Patrol Intelligence Unit about a year to figure out what we were doing. They sent us a message through one of our attorneys: "We know what you guys are up to. Stop it or we will indict you."

I was pastor of the Southside congregation. We declared the church a sanctuary for Central American refugees. And a movement started. Eventually we got the government to recognize these folks as refugees. But I got three federal felony convictions along the way.

Did you serve time?

No, I just got five years' probation. And I've been involved with the border ever since.

Let's head to the border.

Above: Arizona's Sonoran Desert. John says, "It takes four days to walk from Nogales, Mexico, to Tucson, Arizona, on a good, fast trip. But if there are old people, it can take forever. We've known of people walking in circles for eight days, completely lost."

Opposite: A Border Patrol officer.

The Fence. Steel posts are sunk in concrete three feet into the ground. Tunnels are dug four feet under it.

Above: John says, "Towers with surveillance equipment were intended to track walkers across the valley. After $1.2 billion was spent on this initiative, the sensors never worked."

Opposite: At the end of the day, the Border Patrol hooks a tire to the back of a vehicle and drives along the fence line to clear the area of footprints. In the morning, they count footprints from the previous night. This works.

Right: Footprints on the trail point to Tucson.

Below: Empty water jugs. Black jugs are used because they are not detectable at night.

Opposite: A spiderweb of trails crisscrosses through the mountains. People are crossing. Everybody's moving.

"*¡Buenos días!*" Kathryn calls to the migrants. "*Somos amigos. Tenemos agua, comida, medicinas. Llámanos si necesitan ayuda.*" ["Good morning! We are friends. We have water, food, medicines. Let us know if you need help."] No one answers.

No More Deaths/*No Más Muertes* campsite. Crossers get water, food, and medical care from volunteers. "We only see people who need our help. If they have food and water, we don't see them," says John. Today is a good day. No one comes out of the shadows.

Above: Clean clothes donated by Arizona citizens. There is also a phone available to call families back home.

Right: Some captured walkers are sent back to Mexico. Others go to a detention center.

Portrait: P—

WE SAW A RABBIT
P——

When P—— was thirteen years old, she walked through the Sonoran mountains and desert. Her father, now living in New York, had paid for her, her eighteen-year-old sister, and her six-year-old half brother to cross the border and live with him in the United States. Their crossing was not exactly what he had paid for.

We bought new clothes for the journey: dark-blue jeans, a black shirt, and a dark-blue jacket. Even though we're not supposed to wear bright colors, because someone could see us, my new shoes were pink and black. I loved those shoes. They were the first pair of good shoes I ever had. Before, I only wore *huaraches*.

The day we left home we bought food, mostly junk food. A guide picked us up at our house and got us to Puebla, about two hours away. There we had hamburgers and juice. Then we took a three-hour airplane ride to Chihuahua. They gave us small sandwiches on the plane. In Chihuahua we bought more junk food for the eight-hour bus ride to Nogales, Mexico.

We went to a hotel that was more like a private house and stayed there for two nights. The two *coyotes* who would take us across the border wanted to wait for more people to arrive. At five in the afternoon, when the sun was going down, we left. The first guide, the one who had brought us to the house, was not allowed to leave the house until he had gotten word that we had arrived in Arizona. If we got caught or needed to come back to Mexico, he would return us to our village. The two *coyotes* who would be guiding us to the U.S. were supposed to keep in cell-phone contact with the original guy back at the house.

We were told we were going to walk about forty-five minutes and someone was going to pick us up on the other side of the border. But that wasn't true. It took four days.

DAY ONE

The *coyotes* said that my sister and I would walk but my brother would go in a van with two other little kids. That didn't happen either. I think the police showed up and the driver ran away, leaving the kids in the van. I never found out if this happened on the Mexican side or the U.S. side. My brother ended up in an orphanage back in Mexico. We were already walking and didn't know anything about this.

Before we left, the *coyote* gave us some kind of ham, something I had never seen before. It looked so nasty. I hated it. My sister and I had one gallon and two two-liter bottles of water. They told us to leave the two liters because we were going to walk fast.

They drove us to a spot in the desert and told us to get out of the car. When we got out, we met twelve other people who were coming with us. They were in their twenties and thirties, a lot older than me. Most were by themselves and most were men. There was one family — a girl and her dad.

We all climbed and then jumped a three-foot fence. It wasn't the border fence. It was for cattle. We were still in Mexico. As we walked, my sister and I changed the load back and forth; sometimes I carried the water, and sometimes I carried the food. The *coyote* carried his own stuff.

After about five minutes' walking, we saw people with big guns. Their faces were covered. They came from nowhere. I was like, "What's going on?" I was terrified. Who are they? Are they perverts? Are they going to do something to us? One guy told us to go with them.

"What?"

The guy who had his face covered and the guy who was guiding us took us to a hiding place because we were too close to the road. It was like a cave by a dry riverbed. They told us to give them our money and jewelry. We had to give up whatever valuables we had; otherwise they were going to kill us. We didn't have jewelry, but my sister had some money. I was scared because we'd heard from the other people who tried to cross about the *pandillas* who rape girls and sometimes kill men.

They came toward me. "Give us the money. Otherwise we are going to get it from you!"

"She's with me. Don't touch her!" My sister jumped in front of me. She gave them all the money we had. They made us take off our shoes to see if there was money hidden. When they didn't find more money, they left us alone. They didn't touch us. The other girl had a lot of jewelry on her neck. She said she wasn't going to give it to them. The guy put his hand right on her chest and grabbed all her jewelry. I was shocked that he would touch her like that.

One guy didn't want to give them his money. They pulled his pants down! Then they pulled down all the guys' pants to see if they were hiding money. Oh, my God! I turned away, and my sister turned too. And then they pulled down their underwear! They didn't do it to the girls, thank God.

The conclusion that we came to was that these masked guys were part of the same gang as the *coyote* who was bringing us across.

Our guide said, "Let's go!" and we started walking again. There were lots of hills. We went up and down and up again. We didn't walk on paths. We walked through the bushes. We were walking really fast, and the people in front of us were not careful about those behind them. The branches snapped at us and hit our faces. No one helped each other. I got little scratches on my face because I was in front of my sister. My sister said she couldn't walk in front because she needed to be sure I wasn't left behind. And it was getting dark. It was really dark.

> *By now P—'s pink-and-black shoes were streaked with dust and dirt. She and her sister had no money. In spite of this, she was happy. Why?*

Because when I was in Mexico, I did not go to school. For me this was like a dream. I'm going to America, where I can go to school. I'm going to be a professional. I wanted this opportunity so badly. And I wanted to see my father again. We never had a good father-and-daughter relationship, but still, he was my father. Back in Mexico, when I would ask my father if I could go to school, he'd say, "Whatever your grandmother decides." My grandmother was not going to send me to school. That was it! I said to my father, "But I really, really want to go to school."

"No. You're not going to school, because when you're seventeen or eighteen you will become pregnant. You will have sons and daughters and get married." He assumed that's what would happen to me. That's not what I wanted.

"No, I'm not going to do that. I will stay in school." I begged him.

"No. Your grandmother decided. Stop thinking about it."

"Okay." I stopped thinking about it. But when my father said we could come here, my older sister was like, "No, why would I want to go there? I don't want to go there." I'm like, "Please, please, let's go!" It was my big chance.

My sister finally agreed, not just because I pleaded with her. It's more complicated. When I was six years old, my mother died. My father remarried and moved to New Jersey. His wife didn't want to stay in New Jersey, so she came back to Mexico with their son, my little brother, and lived with us. After a while she got together with my father's brother.

My uncle thought he was all-powerful, like a king. Most of the people in the village were scared of him. Even my grandma was scared of her son.

My uncle would hit us. He used a lot of bad words. One time when we were making *frijoles,* he came into the kitchen and started saying, *"¡Estúpidas, estúpidas, estúpidas!"* He made us feel bad. We had very low self-esteem anyway, and for him to say that made it worse. He was drunk, really drunk. He tried to slap me, but my sister blocked him. She got hit in the lip. Her lip turned dark purple. He tried to hit her again. I ran behind him, jumped on his back, and pulled his hair. My sister got the big spoon to make the *frijoles* and started hitting him with it. *Whack! Whack! Whack!* Then we ran from the kitchen to our room. He ran after us. He kicked and kicked the door, trying to open it, but we moved furniture and put a chunk of wood against the door so he couldn't get in.

Finally my uncle left and went to my grandma's room. At that time she had a problem with her ankle and couldn't walk. She hurt it riding the donkey to the village. We didn't know what to do. Would he do something bad to our grandma? Should we protect her? Should we run away? We looked out the window and saw him sitting outside. That was our chance to leave. We went to my aunt's house nearby. My aunt and uncle weren't there, but we stayed with our cousins.

When my aunt and uncle returned home, they saw my sister's purple lip. *"¿Qué pasó?"* They wanted to know what happened. My aunt said that her brother was becoming more and more violent and that we had to get out. This happened in late January or February. In March, we started the walk.

Nighttime in the Desert

It was dark, and we heard all kinds of animals. That didn't scare me much, not like the *pandillas,* because I was used to snakes and animals. Since my mother died, I'd had to take care of my grandma's cows. So from the age of six, I was taking care of twenty cows. I had to take them out to eat in the hills and stay with them all day. I think that's why she didn't want me to go to school.

We finally got to rest in a ravine. While we rested, I looked up at the moon. I thought about my mom. The moon is kind of like my mom. I cried to the moon because I thought life was unfair. The girl who married my dad was a really mean person. She was totally not like my mom. My mom was very kind. Everyone in the village said so. When my father's second wife physically abused us, I would talk to the moon to feel better.

Just as everyone was going to sleep, a man came running toward us. He came to our ravine and said, "*La inmigración* is going to get me. *¡La inmigración! ¡La inmigración!* They are following me." We were standing, ready to run, which was weird because we were still in Mexico. "Don't worry. They won't get any of you," he said. "They just want me."

"Do you want water? Do you want something to eat?" we asked.

"No. No. I'm okay." He kept talking to us. "How are you doing? How long have you been walking?"

We just looked at him. He wasn't young. He was, like, twenty-eight. After four or five minutes, he said, "I have to look for my bag." He walked away, pretending that he was looking for his bag.

I forgot to say that before this guy arrived, two other men came by. They were part of the Mexican military, looking for people with drugs. They sat with us awhile. These two soldiers had big rifles, but they were so friendly. They said, "No, no, no, don't worry. We're not looking for people; we're looking for drugs." They asked us, "So, are you going to go to the United States? How long does it take to get there?" Then they continued on their patrol.

A while later, the two soldiers returned. With them was the guy who had shouted, "*¡La inmigración!*" Their rifles were focused at the top of the guy's head. "What do you have in the bag?" they screamed at him.

"Nothing."

"Where's the other bag? Do you have the other bag?"

"No. There is not another bag."

The soldiers started taking things out of the bag. Jewelry. Belts. Cell phones. Money. One of the soldiers said, "Call your other person and tell them to come here. Don't say nothing, or I will kill you."

So the guy called the other person. "You know I'm already here with these people. You can come."

A second guy showed up with a second bag. Inside was a blanket. The soldiers explained that they used it when they raped people. Thank goodness the soldiers were there, or we don't know what would have happened to us. I'm still traumatized by that.

The soldiers said that these two guys had raped a girl a day before. They knew these guys were still in the area.

Then they said to us, "Who wants the jewelry? Who wants the belts?"

"We don't want nothing," one of the guys said. None of us wanted what didn't belong to us. The people who owned these things were walkers, just like us. We knew what it felt like to be robbed of everything. We all said no.

It's crazy what the soldiers did to those two guys. They took them somewhere in the brush and took away all their clothes. Then they hit them with branches that have thorns, like rose branches. Then they let them go, but without their clothes.

The soldiers told us about it when they returned. We laughed and laughed. Then the soldiers stayed with us all night to be sure we'd be safe.

DAY TWO

At five in the morning we woke up and started walking again. Walking. Walking. We went through more mountains and more mountains. They seemed to never end. The soldiers told us that there are train tracks at the actual border. They escorted us all the way to the American border. They didn't guide us, but they walked with us. They weren't trying to get us across as much as they were scared that these guys would come back and hurt us. We walked fast from five a.m. to noon without a break.

When we reached the train tracks, the soldiers said, "This is the actual border. We cannot cross from the Mexican side. You must go on your own. Nothing will happen to you. It's more dangerous on the Mexican side." We just had to cross the railroad tracks and we would be in America.

The soldiers explained, "We cannot cross to the American side. United States and Mexican patrols respect each other."

We thanked them, said good-bye, and crossed the tracks. We felt nothing different because it looked exactly the same. And we still had to walk.

We saw two helicopters. "Get down in the bushes!" the guide shouted, hunching down. We hid. Once the helicopters left we started walking again.

When we stopped for the night, we got to eat. I couldn't eat. I didn't feel hungry, and I didn't like that ham. I just drank water.

That night it was so cold. We had only the clothes we were wearing. My sister said, "Let's hug each other so we don't feel that cold." But still I was cold, too cold to sleep. We couldn't light a fire because the Border Patrol would see it.

DAY THREE

This day we had to run. We came to a metal wire that if you touched it, it would set off an alarm. So we had to lie down and inch our way under it one at a time. We dug some dirt out so the larger people could fit under it.

Then we started running more. We went through small bushes. The dirt changed to sand. Sand just kills your feet. Sand gets you really tired.

There were crosses all around us where people had died. And we also saw bones of people. Some had their shoes and the bones.

My sister wanted to stay there. "You are crazy!" I said. She was so tired. We weren't just walking through sand; we were running through the sand. We were down to a very little bit of water. I was really thirsty, but my sister was like, "I want to stay here. We have no more water. My feet are tired. And I'm thirsty."

"So drink the last water."

"No, that's for you."

"No. Drink it. Drink it."

"Okay." And then she drank it. We rested a little bit and then went on. There was another guy behind us. He was so slow. We left him. We never saw him again. I felt sad because he was not the only one who was left behind. Two others were left before that.

I saw more crosses and more dead people. I wanted to cry, but I thought I better keep positive for my sister. I told my sister, "YOU'RE

GOING TO KEEP WALKING!" She was like, "No, I don't want to walk anymore. I'm so tired."

"Give me the bag of food. You're going to walk!" The people and *coyotes* were way ahead of us. We had to run to catch up. Then we saw that the group stopped, so we started to take our time. We soon saw that they stopped because they had to cross an expressway. We had to cross to the other side and there were lots of cars going really fast.

My sister said, "You go first."

"No, you go first."

"No. You go first." I was afraid if I went first she'd stay there because she was so tired. So we went together.

After we crossed the road, we waited for the people to pick us up. We waited. And waited. They never picked us up.

We had no food and no water. We slept there that night.

DAY FOUR

When we woke up, we went looking for water. We saw horses and cows. We went to see if there was some water for them. But the cows and horses didn't have water either. We didn't take milk from the cows because people might see us stealing and call immigration.

We came to another ravine, a big, deep one. When we looked down, we saw a long line of people sitting along the sides. Our *coyotes* knew their *coyotes*. They invited us to sit with them. They had food. They had water. They had donuts. They had all this good stuff. And they shared everything with us.

I think one of the men who was guiding us was a drug addict. He left to go smoke marijuana a little ways away. There must have been cameras around because the immigration patrol saw him. Or maybe they saw the smoke. I don't know.

And what did he do? He ran to us rather than away from us. So the patrol found all of us. We were caught.

Our *coyote* threw his cell phone in the dirt. I thought why is he leaving his cell phone? When I reached for it, he shouted at me, "Just leave it there!"

The patrol told us to take off earrings, rings, and shoelaces and put them in our bags. My sister and I only had shoelaces. Then they lined us up and put handcuffs on some of us. They did it to my sister but not to me. They put us in a van. The girls were in one van, and the boys were in another van.

I was scared. Those officers had guns. I said, "What's going on?"

"Oh, we're going to spend a night in jail," another woman said.

"No way," I said. "Jail? Me?"

When we got to the immigration station, they threw us in the jail. Jail! Me! The guard kept the men separated from the women. One guard, with pale skin and blue eyes, said, "Put your shoes on and, like a rabbit, run back to Mexico." He wasn't so nice.

I was hungry. I asked another guard, "Can I get something to eat?"

"Sure. Sure. I have some cookies and juice." That guard was nice to us. He had a Spanish look.

My sister was taken out to get her fingerprints taken. I stayed behind. It made me nervous to be away from her. When she returned, the guard took us to a door of the immigration station.

Crossing the Border

The guard opened a door. We walked down a small hallway and went through a kind of turnstile, like in the subway. We were back in Mexico. We had walked so long to get to the States. Returning to Mexico took five seconds. We couldn't believe it.

Once we were back in Mexico, we saw a taxi. We told the driver the name of the house where we had stayed. "Oh, I know them," he said. He drove us back to the house and the guy who was waiting to hear from us paid him. When we arrived at the house, he told us that our brother was lost.

"WHAT???"

They didn't know where he was, so he assumed that he was lost. We made him call whoever was in charge and asked him to search all the orphanages. It took two days to find the right orphanage. Even though they found my brother, we had to wait another fifteen days to get him out of the orphanage. My father was not there to sign the forms saying that my brother was his son. And he did not trust his second wife to do it. So he had to pay a politician from our district to go and get my brother out of the orphanage.

My sister and I wondered what would have happened to our brother if we had been successful getting across to the other side. Would he be lost forever? How could we live with that? Maybe getting caught happened for a reason.

When our brother finally got out, he was so happy to see us. He said, "I didn't know if I was ever going to find you again. I didn't know anyone. I was scared I would stay there my whole life and not be able to see you again."

My father was really mad at the people he had paid to bring us to America. "Why did you separate them? And why did you make them walk for four days?"

The people were like, "We're going to send them now, but we need more money. They are not going to walk that much." We didn't know if we should believe them. They lied to us the first time.

We asked my father if we could do something else. He said, "I just paid a lot of money to them. I want you guys here. I'm going to give them the money, because if I don't, they might hurt you. I don't want that to happen."

Two days after my brother got out of the orphanage, we were ready to walk again. But this time we took a cab to the fence, the real border fence. We had to do the crossing by ourselves, though. We were our own guides. They explained how to do it. "You go here, you walk like this, when you get to this place, take off your jackets, and walk to Fourteenth Street. A white car will be waiting for you — or you wait for the white car." The guide said it would take no more than twenty-five minutes.

P— explained that their coyote organization offered two rates for bringing people across the border. The cheaper rate was for the slow, four-day walk through the mountains and across the desert. The expensive, fast rate meant climbing a nearby fence. The thing is, P—'s

On the Mexican side, the fence was about ten feet high, and on the American side it was about thirteen feet high. On the American side they took dirt from the bottom to make the fence taller. The *coyote* put up a ladder on the Mexican side of the fence and we climbed up. But the only way to get down on the American side was to jump!

I was afraid to jump. I held tight to the top of the fence. The *coyote* yelled, "LET GO! LET GO! Someone's going to see you!"

"I'm not letting go. The fence is too high."

"Someone's going to see you!" I didn't want to jump, until my hands got tired. That's when I let go.

My sister took my brother with her. My sister jumped. Then, when my brother jumped, she caught him in the air.

It was three in the afternoon and people saw us, but they didn't say anything.

We went into the nearby bushes and crawled a long way. We were afraid to stand because more people would be able to see us. We saw a rabbit. In my culture that means good luck. We took off our jackets and threw them away because they were dirty and old and kind of messed up from our crawling. We had nice clothes under the jacket. A dog started barking, and that's when more people came out and saw us. But none of them said a word.

We stood up and walked like nice people until we reached Fourteenth Street. The white car was there.

AFTER . . .

The long road to an education did not end with the white car. By the time P— arrived in the States, her father was living in Brooklyn and working for a friend who owned a construction company.

I was excited to be here with my dad because I thought that finally we could be a real father and daughter. But he still didn't want me to go to school. He wanted me to go to work and help support the family. I couldn't understand why he was still thinking like that. I thought that if I asked and I asked, that maybe he would change his mind. But he still said no. I convinced my sister to help me sign up for school.

I was placed in eighth grade and began learning English. After school I had to take care of my brother, clean the house, and make the meals. Once everyone went to bed, I did my homework.

I did well in school and made lots of friends. Even though my father had to admit that I was a serious student, he refused to look at my report cards, and he would never go to parent-teacher meetings. At least I was on the way to an education. But then . . .

An Accident

When I was in ninth grade, going into tenth grade, my dad got hurt while he was working his construction job. He couldn't work and make enough money to support us. He told me to look for a full-time job and quit school to help support the family. I said that I would do part-time work after school. He became very angry. He said, "In my culture, having your own opinion is considered disrespectful." My dad yelled and yelled. He said that if I wanted to keep living with him, I must follow his rules.

One day, on the way to the laundry, I saw my father's boss. He was such a good friend, I called him my "uncle." I told him that my father still insisted that I quit school. My uncle offered me a part-time job on his construction site so that I could continue my education. I thought that would help. Still my father said no. Our arguing grew worse. Finally my uncle invited me to move in with him and his wife. My father did not object.

Eventually my uncle taught me carpentry and welding. I began welding on his construction sites and for art installations in Williamsburg, Brooklyn.

When I heard about DACA, I went to an organization that helps young people like me. It's called the Door. And I met my future lawyer, Rebecca McBride.

Rebecca picks up the story: "As P— and I got to talking, I learned that not only was she not living with her father, because of his attempts to pull her out of school so that she could work, but also she was not living with her mom, because she had passed away when P— was just a little girl. I realized then that P— could qualify for a type of humanitarian immigration relief called Special Immigrant Juvenile Status (SIJS). This law exists for children under the age of twenty-one who, among other things, cannot be reunited with one or both parents due to abandonment, abuse, or neglect – which includes refusing to send a child to school. Those who receive SIJSs are also eligible to adjust their status; that is, they can apply for a green card and be on the path toward lawful permanent residency." Rebecca and P— went to court. In time, P—was awarded a green card.

I've become a welder, a teacher, and a student. I work three jobs: one, for my uncle; another, as an assistant teacher at a technical school for young children; and third, working alongside Rebecca at Atlas: DIY to help young immigrants navigate the college application process. I'm in my freshman year of college, studying to become an electrical engineer. When I'm working at my jobs I learn something new. Learning from other people inspires me to be whatever I want to be. I'm very happy.

"I've become a welder, a teacher, and a student."

Portrait: C—

CHAPTER FIVE

UNDER MY SHADOW
C——

C— crossed into the U.S. through the Sonoran Desert and lived near the border, in Arizona. Growing up undocumented kept him in the shadows for most of his life. C— also had another shadow, one that he has revealed to only a few people . . . until now.

My family has a strange tradition. On your birthday — after a certain age — the siblings wake you up with a bucket of cold water. My sixth birthday was my ice bucket year. I remember it clearly because it was the first day of my real life. My birthday is May 8. My father passed away July 18. I came here ten days after that, July 28. It was also the year of self-discovery — the year I realized that I was different. So my sixth birthday was my game changer.

I have eight siblings, two older sisters and six brothers. Big family! The younger of my sisters and my little half brother were lucky to be born in the States.

My older sister is pretty cute and very feminine. When she played with me, she dressed me up in female clothes. I felt more comfortable in those clothes than in my male clothes. Because our parents were working in the States, our grandmother took care of us. She wasn't a kind person. Her way of discipline was to beat the crap out of us. That's how she reacted when I started acting more feminine. I hung out with my neighbor who was a girl. My grandmother didn't like that. She once grabbed a branch from a tree and whipped me. She would tell me to "man up." That was our culture, all that *machismo* and everything.

Mexico–U.S.

Let me tell you about the place where I grew up, Lazaro Cardenas, in Mexico. It's a small place, even smaller than Michoacán, the port city nearby. Our closest neighbor was half a mile away. We lived in a two-room house. The boys slept in one room, and the girls slept in the other room. There was no living room, no kitchen — we cooked outside in a small pit — and of course an outhouse was our bathroom.

I didn't know it at the time, but we were extremely poor. Although I didn't think we suffered for things, there were times when we didn't have enough to eat. That's why my mother and father ventured back and forth between our home in Mexico and the U.S. They were always searching for new ways to make a living. We would go years without seeing them. Before I was born, they worked in Los Angeles, California. My mom was a housekeeper, and my father worked as a dishwasher in a restaurant. Once they made enough money, they returned to Mexico to fix up our house. I was born during one of those periods.

But we soon ran out of money, and my parents migrated back to the U.S., this time to Arizona. They found work in what they were most comfortable doing: my mother cleaned hotel rooms, and my father washed dishes in a restaurant.

My younger brother, an older brother, and my oldest sister went with them. I stayed home with my grandma and the other siblings. My three other older brothers worked in the fields. They grew corn and sugarcane. They had to do it. It was either that or have nothing to eat. I didn't do anything, because I was too little. Those fields were a wedding gift to my father from my grandmother. Later, she took them back. I guess it doesn't matter now. My mom once told me that she was sending money to us and that's why she and my dad were away so long. But I don't ever remember receiving the fruits of their labor.

Unfortunately, this was my father's last trip to the U.S. He was murdered in 1998. It is hard to talk about this. But I want to tell the whole story.

The Trauma

While I was still in Mexico, my dad was killed during a family celebration in Arizona. Usually when the bathroom is full and there's a line, you just go outside. When my father and brother went outside, a car pulled up. An individual popped out and started shooting. My father fell to his death. My brother, who was about five feet away from them, collapsed in horror.

They never caught the man who did this. I heard that he was well known to my family. Another individual from our family helped him get away. I can't name this individual because I don't know who she is for sure. I guess you can say it was a family job.

Back in Mexico, I knew something bad had happened, but at age six, I didn't understand what it was. Everyone was crying. All I knew was my grandma said that my mom was coming back home. I was overjoyed.

A week after my mom returned home, I saw a hearse pull up. I had never seen that type of vehicle in my life. I wanted to see what it was, so I met it where they pulled in. I guess the two drivers needed to make sure the man in the coffin was my dad, so they pulled out the casket and opened it. I was right there. I guess they didn't care about a six-year-old child's emotions. They were strangers and didn't know who I was. I heard them laughing when they drove away.

At first I was confused about the hearse and didn't feel anything. Then my eyes flooded with tears. I don't know. I don't know. I filled up with emotions that I didn't know existed. I didn't know where my mother was. My grandmother was getting the chairs ready for the wake. I had this idea that if anybody saw me cry, they would think of me as weak and brittle. I forced the emotions out of me. It was a weird, weird situation. Now I know that not showing your emotions is a bad way to live.

After the funeral, which I do not remember at all, the big question was who was going to take care of the family. It had to be my mom. My mother realized that the only place where she could earn enough to support everyone was back in the States.

Money was running out, and she had to do something fast. There was never a question about *what* to take, because we had so little. The question was *who* to take.

My mom decided to leave behind my three older brothers and take my California-born sister and me with her. My brothers didn't want our mom to leave. They later said that they felt abandoned.

My mom came up with a plan to cross the border. My *tía* from Arizona agreed to meet my U.S.-born sister and me at the border. She would use her son's passport to get me across. Not everything went according to plan.

What's Your Name?

When the guard asked me my name, I was supposed to say that I was my cousin. But I had always been told to be honest. Never lie! Never steal! How could I give the wrong name at the crossing? That was a lie.

"Is this your name?" The guard pointed to my cousin's passport.

"No. My name is F——." I gave him my formal, long name, rather than the short version I always use. They sent my *tía* back to Mexico with a warning not to try to take me across.

We returned to the hotel where my mom was waiting to hear that we got across safely. When she saw all three of us arrive at the hotel, she knew immediately what I had done. Oh, was she pissed! This may sound awful, but even at age six, I knew right from wrong, and here was my family telling me to lie. I wouldn't do it. I would rather walk across the desert with my mom and not lie than make it safely across in one or two hours by lying.

After I ruined the plan, my mom had no choice but to take me with her on the walk. We left my sister and aunt in Nogales. They could cross legally.

My mother carried me most of the way. I guess this is why I love her so much. Even though I had a rough childhood, and she wasn't the loving mother that a typical child here in the U.S. expects, I love her unconditionally. And even though she doesn't express it, I knew — and I know — that she loves me, because she carried me across the desert.

I only remember one night of the journey. We were crossing a hill. You know the crosses that symbolize people who had died? I saw many of them — so many of them. It was only two weeks after my father's funeral, and I knew what the crosses symbolized. We had to sleep by the crosses. That made me remember my father in the coffin. I was so scared lying in the shadows of those crosses.

We slept during the day and walked when the sun was down. It was ominous and horrific. I don't remember walking except when my mom put me down so she could rest. I know it was hard for her. Because of me she still has a bad back. I believe we ran out of water, because my lips were chapped. They were chapped and red, and the skin was falling off. I also remember being picked up along a highway by some individual. He drove us to my aunt's house.

When we rendezvoused at my aunt's house, there was a big family reunion. My sister and brothers, who had not gone to Mexico for our father's funeral, were there. Everyone was so happy to see us. I didn't see what the big deal was. I rarely talk about this part of my life.

School?

I did not understand why I had to go to school. Why was I going to spend half my day in this place? Why? I didn't go to school in Mexico.

While my mom was in the office signing me up, I ran outside and hid under a car. She ran out, looking for me. The principal ran out. Everyone in the office made such a big deal about it. A teacher tried to pull me out. "Hey, come over here . . ." but I didn't understand what he was saying. I just put my head down and closed my eyes. It was scandalous.

My first teacher was very unconventional. He would reward the class with candy or whatnot. My cavities thanked him. I'm kidding. We would play bingo a lot. A lot! As a child, I thought, Oh my God, this is heaven. Now I think, really? *Really?* What were you thinking? He didn't teach anything. He ended up getting fired. There were standardized tests, and a lot of us failed. I was one who failed. It was *terrible!*

During my elementary-school years, we lived with my uncle, his wife, and their two kids. They are two years younger than me. I didn't have the urge to develop other friendships, because if I wanted to play, I could play with them. They were in different schools, which is odd because we lived in the same house.

I was bullied in school but not because I didn't speak English well. I was bullied because of my feminine characteristics. My walk was different from the other kids' walks. My mannerisms were different from the other kids' mannerisms. I just didn't belong. I felt like a red piece in a green puzzle. I felt as if I was living under my own shadow.

Ever since I was six years old, I preferred wearing female clothing to male clothing. I tried to hide it by acting more masculine, because I didn't want to raise a red flag in public or in front of my family. I probably didn't fool anybody.

When I turned eight, I hung out with little rascals, the bad kids. I tried to prove to myself that I could be like them. It wasn't genuine, because I felt so uncomfortable. And I still feel uncomfortable; actually, I don't feel like I'm in my own skin at this point.

Not only was I hiding my sexuality; I was hiding my undocumented status too. My mom would say, "Don't say you walked across the border. Don't say you are here illegally." And on top of that was "Walk like a man!" I felt so misunderstood. So when I started hanging out with the bad kids, I felt even more out of place. I was faking it to make it. I knew I could only take so much. Eventually my true self, my genuine true self, was going to come out. But in the meantime, I continued to hide under the two shadows. And remember, I don't like lying. So I pushed everyone aside and stayed by myself. It was lonely. It really was.

The High Road

In 2000, when I was eight, we moved to the projects. They are the worst. I was headed down the wrong road, but I was stopped before I got into really bad trouble.

Ages eight to twelve were my mischief years. I hung out with a bad crowd, the drinking crowd. I wasn't drinking, but I stayed out till one a.m., two a.m. They were stealing too. I could not do that. They weren't undocumented like me. They were all citizens.

There were a couple of instances when they egged cars. If the driver of the car went after them, their adrenaline would kick in as they ran. It was a high that only mischief could satisfy. I, on the other hand, did not have a gift for crime. The first egg I threw was the last.

I got caught. It must have been fate, because getting caught saved me. I was walking home after the egging, and there was my mother outside with my sister and one of my brothers. With them were the people in the vehicle that I had egged. What happened was a bystander who knew me witnessed the incident. He led the couple to my apartment. I was in big trouble. My mom was extremely angry. She hit me. She whipped me with a belt. A lot of Hispanic families believe in harsh punishments when it comes to their kids. I don't have any animosity toward my mom — I knew I had done wrong — but if I had a kid, I would never hit him.

Fortunately, the couple didn't press charges. This was a huge learning experience for me. I didn't want to see my mother angry. I knew she was going through a lot. By this time, my older brothers were living with us. My mother had walked each one across the desert. They were always getting in trouble. They had all dropped out of high school because they were getting bullied. They were teased because they had thick accents and didn't know the simplest English words. When they read out loud, the other kids laughed at them. They were traditional Latinos, new to the country, with high expectations. The teasing really got to them. Finally, they just gave up and dropped out.

Every single time my brothers got in trouble, my mom bailed them out. I feel like she was a source of their problems. My oldest brother is thirty-one now. He's the one who witnessed my father's murder. He has epileptic seizures. He was taking medicine, but drugs became his gateway to being happy. He fell into addiction and ended up in prison. Eventually he was deported back to Mexico. My two other older brothers followed the wrong path and were deported too.

After they were deported, my mom became very close and tender with me. And isn't life funny? It takes a tragedy to bring people together.

Coming Out

People don't know if you are undocumented unless they ask. Whenever someone asked if I had my papers, I was quick on my feet and changed the subject. But when they asked if I was gay, I was taken aback and didn't have a quick answer. And it wasn't only what they asked me that was upsetting; it was what I knew they were saying behind my back.

At that time I considered myself a guy who's gay. There were times, though, when I'd look at myself in the mirror and think, I'm in the wrong body. I tried to fight it because of my family, because of my Mexican tradition. I tried to adapt a mind-set to think like a guy. It soon became evident that this was not working, and I became depressed.

Then something good happened. In my sophomore year, I started to be a little bit happy. That was because of Y——. In French class,

Y— walked over to my desk and said, "Hey, what's your name?" Her simple recognition took me out of my shell and made me more comfortable speaking with other people. Unfortunately, after some years she moved, and we've lost contact. Life goes on. Thank you, Y—.

After Y—'s kindness, I became more confident and started networking. That's when I met Melissa and M—. Melissa and M— were best friends. Melissa is a documented Latina. M— is an undocumented Latina.

Melissa went to my school. M— went to a different school. Melissa and I were both in the closet. M— was out. M— was so flamboyant. She was a free spirit who wasn't afraid to admit that she was a lesbian. I envied her. I wished I could be like her and not care who knew about my sexuality. She became a symbol of what our lives could be. Through Melissa and M— I started hanging out with a lot of people who were comfortable with their sexuality. They were the reason why I came out to my mom.

Dear Mom

First, I needed my sisters' support. I told my oldest sister first. She was in her midtwenties at the time. She had already figured me out, of course. She said, "I love you no matter what." It was awesome. Her husband has a gay cousin, so she understood the notion that being gay wasn't a disease. I got her approval.

My older sister told our second sister. She said, "If Mom kicks you out, you can live here." That was what I needed to hear.

I thought coming out to Mom would be a train wreck. I was right. I wrote a letter to her because I couldn't tell her in person. I wrote the note in Spanish. I had to teach myself to write Spanish because by then I was only speaking English. Basically I said that I didn't care what she thought about me, because she made it evident over the years that she disapproved of me. And since I had my sisters' support, it didn't matter what she thought. Of course I did care; I cared so much because I loved her so much. I needed her approval.

"She wanted to know who made me this way."

I think both of us were heartbroken, because I didn't choose my words wisely. I say "no regrets," but I should have written it in a different tone. I could have been softer. Her first reaction was to laugh. That's her way of coping. I don't like being emotional in front of people, so I laughed too. I thought, okay, I'd join in the joke. A big joke, apparently.

Her second reaction was a question: "Who made you gay?" That was like plunging a sword in my heart. It's this stigma in Hispanic culture that you're not born gay; you're made gay. I tried hard to explain it to her and thought I was making progress. Then she asked, "Who touched you?" And I'm, like, oh my God, when it comes to speaking to Mom, it's like speaking to a wall. No matter if she knows that she's wrong, once she says something, she sticks with it. She laughed. She mocked me. She wanted to know who made me this way. I said, "Nobody made me. I'm just like this." There was some sadness in her eyes, because she knew she couldn't do anything about me. I went to my room. She stayed in the living room.

I knew she was worried about my welfare, though, because she had my sister pick me up after school. She thought I might become a runaway. That's how I knew she cared.

Since then, we haven't talked about it. To this day, we do not talk about it. Gay marriage is legal in Mexico. However, it's taken society such a long, long time to adjust to the fact that people are born gay, not made gay. Also, they automatically feel you have AIDS because you are gay. Even my sister said be careful because of AIDS.

By my senior year, my mother had remarried. I didn't feel comfortable with my stepfather. He's a traditional Mexican guy, and he doesn't accept my lifestyle. He came into the picture about a year after my father's passing. My aunts thought it was time for my mom to meet someone. How do older Mexicans mingle? At the *club de bailé,* a dance club. He wasn't part of my life until he and my mother bought a house together. And they had a child, my half brother, who I love with all my heart.

My stepfather was home a lot, so I moved in with my friend Melissa. My mother thought I was living with my older sister. To be honest, I was living with Melissa's brother. We've been together for three years.

DREAMers

During my senior year, people from the Arizona DREAM Act Coalition did a presentation at my school about undocumented immigrants. I connected to what they said and joined their group. It was the first time I acknowledged that I was undocumented. I was a little fearful at first. Very few people knew this about me.

After graduation, the question was, what now? I had no idea where my life was going. I was unemployed. The legal system was against me. I couldn't afford college. I found a simple job that paid above minimum wage. I worked the graveyard shift at a grocery store, cleaning the floors. Honestly, I am not meant for manual labor. One machine resembled a bulky lawnmower. The other one was thin with a handle at the top that connected to the motor and rotating fibers used to clean the waxed floors. Oh, my God, the machinery was so heavy, any miscalculation and a shelf would topple over. I worked from ten p.m. to seven a.m.

I was already depressed and stressed, and a night job made it even worse. I couldn't sleep during the day, so I only got about four hours of zzz's. This was not a life. I needed to get back to my community. I wanted to make a difference, not spend my life doing jobs like cutting bushes. My partner saw the disparity in my life and paid for my first community college class, English 101. That class alone cost over nine hundred dollars. My partner is really supportive. He has a good job because he's documented.

In 2012, President Obama announced the DACA program. Maybe there was a future for me after all! I researched how much full tuition would cost and what kinds of part-time jobs would help pay for it. But then the governor of Arizona didn't allow DACAmented students to get the lower in-state tuition or even to get a state driver's license at that time. The sheriff began profiling Latinos. My friend Maria had a rosary in the window of her car, and she was pulled over just for that. That was like a slap in the face. And I hit a wall once again.

During the 2012 elections, the DREAMers were looking for volunteers to go door-to-door to remind people to vote. I went with a DREAMer named D——. She told me about QUIP [Queer Undocumented Immigrant

Project]. There was a new chapter starting up, and she asked me if I was interested in getting involved.

A week later, I went to the meeting, and then went to every meeting. It wasn't easy to express my sexuality in public. I felt a little derailed by the idea. But I love being part of QUIP. Sometimes I'm so busy with them I don't have time for other things. For example, I haven't seen my mother all week.

Even though I'm a little more comfortable being out, I'm not out as transgender. That's my ongoing issue. There are so many considerations. Since my mom is not comfortable with the whole gay thing, this will be another layer to the cake of disappointment. I feel as if my life is a never-ending battle against shadows. I've come out of the shadows about being undocumented. I've come out of the shadows about being gay. After all this, I'm still fighting gender identity. And that's where I am now. But, you know, I'm a fighter. And no shadow is ever going to stop me.

PART TWO

TWISTS AND

TURNS

Portrait: J—

CHAPTER SIX

LUCKY BREAKS
J——

"I'm here! I'm here! Exactly on time."

Climbing the steps to the studio for his interview, water in hand, J—— talks at breakneck speed about how, when he was thirteen years old, he came from Accra, Ghana, to America. The sound of his voice is like music, silver bells and a slide trombone.

"Wait! Wait! You're going too fast. The recorder isn't even on."

"Hahahahaha!"

Unlike the other people in this book, J—— was brought to America under deceitful circumstances.

"Where do you want to start?"

"Let's start with a knock on the door."

PART ONE: Going to School in America

Someone came to the door. When I opened it, a man said, "Does Mr. X live here?"

"Yeah, he's my father. He lives here."

I called to my father, "Dad, you have a visitor."

I'm the oldest son of six children, four boys and two girls. I was in the living room with my sister, playing a dice game we call *ludu*. My mom was eating supper, and my father was reading the newspaper. Usually we eat together as a family, but this night was different.

The man at the door came from the United States to visit my family. We called him Bruce. Well, my parents called him Bruce. I called him Mr. Bruce. They were happy when they saw each other. He was an old friend. My brothers and sisters came out to meet him.

My father told him that we were having financial problems, and he said, "Let me know if you need any help. I'll help you."

After that day, things changed. Usually my dad and I talked about soccer and everything. But after the visit from Mr. Bruce, he didn't talk at all. He was quiet. He was thinking. I couldn't ask him what he was thinking. I mean, I could ask, but I didn't want to know. I was afraid he would say that he didn't know how to pay my school fees. I didn't want to hear that, so I didn't ask.

Two or three weeks later, my dad told me, "You're going to the States." I was really surprised. He explained that they could no longer afford to pay for my schooling. He explained that Mr. Bruce would take me to the States with him. My father said, "You can go to high school in New York."

I said, "Okay, I don't mind." I was happy.

My family's home is part of a large compound in a poor suburb. According to my parents, our house was built by one of our great-grandfathers. There are twelve buildings in the compound. It's a square of houses, but the fourth side has a gate. The bathrooms are outside for all to share. I played soccer with my cousins and friends in the center of the square. Many kids lived in the compound.

Our house had two bedrooms. My parents slept in one room, and my sisters shared the other. At first the boys slept in bunk beds in the living room, but when the beds fell apart, we put the mattresses on the floor.

My dad invested all his money in our private school education. To get a good education in Ghana, you have to go to a private school. They don't teach anything in the public schools. There is no supervision. I was a very good student and skipped two grades.

My father was a subcontractor on a farm. When the farm went out of business, he lost his job, and we faced many financial challenges. My dad ran up debts, trying to pay for all our schooling.

Like my mom, I'm a funny person. I'm very goofy. I like making jokes. I make good animal noises. There were no animals around my house in Ghana, so when people heard animal noises, they knew I was around. Even now I do it. But as the oldest boy in the family, it's my responsibility to take care of my sisters — even if they married a rich man. That meant I had to be successful. I had to be serious.

Flying Through Clouds

I came to the U.S. with two shirts, two pairs of pants, two pairs of underwear, toothpaste, and a toothbrush. That's it.

> *Later, when J— went to an American court about his immigration status, he recalled other events in his life. His affidavit states, "I remember my mom was crying as she said good-bye. In the days leading up to when I left, my dad would pull me aside and remind me to be a 'good boy' and to do whatever Bruce told me to do because he was doing a very nice thing to bring me to the United States."*

At the airport in Ghana, I thought something fishy was going on. They asked Mr. Bruce, "Is this your child?" and he said, "Yeah, he's my son." I didn't say anything. If someone is trying to help you, what can you say?

When we were about to leave, I was only thinking about my family. But once we got on the plane, I stopped thinking about them. We took off, and I felt funny, like butterflies were in my stomach. I was like, what is this? What is that? I thought the plane might fall if I didn't sit still. In my head I was smiling.

Mr. Bruce let me sit next to the window. He was very nice to me. All of a sudden I saw the huge buildings become small objects. I liked it. There were smiles all over my face. I wished I could see my face. When we went through the clouds, I couldn't believe it.

They brought us food two times! I don't remember what it was exactly, but the first meal was good. The second one was something that didn't look so good, and I wouldn't touch it. I asked the flight attendant to bring me water. But the water had lime in it. I thought, is this crazy? We had limes in Ghana but not in the water. In my understanding you don't take acid and fruits until after you eat. That's how I grew up. Mr. Bruce said I should taste it. It tasted good.

After flying through the clouds, I listened to music and checked all the entertainment options that I could watch or listen to. There was so much. I could see how many miles we had flown so far or watch a movie or listen to music. I checked the miles every thirty minutes, and then went back to watching movies. This took all my attention until I realized that we were going down. I think the flight took eleven hours. We left Tuesday and arrived Wednesday.

It was October, and I was cold on the plane. I had on a fleece vest but was still feeling cold. I was used to hot temperatures.

Lucky Break Number One

At JFK Airport, in New York, the customs officer handed me my passport. I put it in my shirt pocket. Mr. Bruce forgot to take it from me. Looking back on my story, it was my first lucky break.

J—'s lawyer explained that had Mr. Bruce taken J—'s passport, he would have been left without any form of identification. Without access to his own documents, J— would have had a harder time leaving what became a perilous situation. Taking away a person's passport is a common act of traffickers.

We arrived at night, and people were still walking in the street, talking and shouting. It was amazing. We went to Mr. Bruce's apartment in Harlem.

As I said, it was October, and school had started in September. So he said, "You can't go to school right now because school is already in session. You have to wait until the first semester is over."

I didn't know anything. In my country there are three school terms — it's a trimester. Until you go to college you have trimesters. I assumed I had to wait till the next semester.

I lived in Mr. Bruce's apartment. The living room had a TV and a comfortable white-and-brown cotton couch. There was one table by a window. There were two bedrooms. I was in one bedroom, and he was in the other. I was sleeping on a mattress on the floor with one pillow and one blanket. The apartment was heated. After all, he was living there too.

The bathroom was very intimidating. The first time I walked in to take a shower, I didn't know about the hot water and the cold water. We had never had a conversation about that. I love water. I didn't read the letters on the tap. I got in and turned one knob on high because I wanted to feel the pressure. Hot water came out in such a force — *WHOOOOSH!*

YEEE-OOOOW! The water burned my head and neck. That shower was a harsh teacher. Now I ask first, "How do I do that?"

When Mr. Bruce went outside, he locked the door so I couldn't go anywhere. I tried to find a way to go outside, but the door would lock on me and I didn't have a key, so I just stayed in the room. I was completely alone. There was a television that I watched all day. I watched musicals and wrestling and basketball. Television is not helpful. It makes you dumb.

When Mr. Bruce came home, he'd just go to his room. He cooked food for himself and whatever was left over I was allowed to eat. I ate by myself. There was always food inside the fridge. We never had conversations.

I didn't know him, so what could I talk to him about? Every day I swept the apartment, but I never went into his room. His door was always locked unless he was there.

Lucky Break Number Two

One day Mr. Bruce came home earlier than usual. I was just sitting there, watching wrestling. Mr. Bruce told me that I couldn't be in the house all day long. He said that I was doing a good job cleaning the apartment, but I was going to start working for his friend as well. He said that if I worked there for a little while, I could go to school.

> From J—'s affidavit: "When Bruce told me I needed to work for his friend before I went to school, that was the first time I thought that maybe he was lying to me and had also lied to my family. I began to realize that Bruce had no supplies or anything for me to go to school with, like a backpack or anything else that would be needed if I actually had class. I was wondering what Bruce had told my dad, and what I should do. Even though I was starting to get suspicious, I think part of me also wanted to believe that Bruce was not a bad man and that everything would turn out okay. So I just told him okay, and Bruce left the room."

I had never worked. In Ghana, I went to school. I thought, this is a different country and maybe there are different rules. I still thought he was somehow trying to help me. Mr. Bruce found a job for me in a store in the Bronx. He bought me a sweatshirt, a one-week MetroCard, and gave me a key to the apartment. The key would later become my second lucky break.

The next Sunday, Mr. Bruce gave me a coat and took me outside to the subway. I hadn't been outside in months, so it was very overwhelming. He took me to the store the first day and then left directions on a piece of paper about how to come home. An African lady called Hagea owned the shop.

She sold reject products, like clothing, from the big stores. I was supposed to be a salesperson. Hagea didn't feed me. She didn't have heat in the store. It was cold there, and all I had to wear that was warm was that sweatshirt. Mr. Bruce had taken back his coat after the first day.

The store had a clock, so I knew that Hagea left around noon and came back around nine at night. During that time, I couldn't leave the store, had nothing to eat, and couldn't even go pee.

I'd go to the store in the morning as early as nine and go home late, sometimes ten thirty. At the end of the first day, she asked me if I knew my way home. I didn't know for sure.

She called a taxi, gave him my address, and gave me fifty dollars to pay the fare. It was the first time I held dollars. FIFTY DOLLARS! I thought every day, fifty dollars! I will be rich. So I fell in love with the job.

The second day, Hagea left the shop and didn't return until eight p.m. It was very boring. And it was so cold in there. By this time it was like winter — November, close to December. The third day was a regular day. Nothing really happened. At three thirty, I was allowed to go out for lunch. I asked a lady who was window-shopping if there was a place to eat nearby. She said there were lots of restaurants around the corner. I found a Sudanese restaurant in the neighborhood and used some of the fifty dollars to pay for my meal. At the restaurant I asked if there was a *masjid* nearby, so I could pray. Did I tell you I'm a Muslim? I am. I'm Muslim.

I tried to pray five times a day, the way I did in Ghana. I tried to do it the best I could, but it wasn't perfect. Mr. Bruce never took me to the *masjid* on Friday night for traditional prayers. He wasn't a Muslim.

By the fourth day, Thursday, I hadn't sold anything to anybody. Hagea became mean. "Nobody comes to the store and buys anything. People come to the store and just go."

She asked if Mr. Bruce told me about my pay, and I told her no.

"Business is slow, as you can see, and I don't know how to pay you. Let's wait a while until business picks up, and I'll pay you all the debt I owe you."

"I don't mind," I said. I still had part of the fifty dollars in my pocket. If I get fifty dollars another day, I will be rich. That first fifty was the only money she ever gave me.

"Are you trying to say I'm bad luck?"

When I came back from my lunch break, she asked me, "What are you doing? I just sold sixteen shirts and dresses and one pair of shoes and you just sit here." She said that I was bad luck, a bad omen.

I said, "What's your impression? Do you think I steal money?"

"No, but how do you work? I came here and sold things. You sold nothing."

I stood up for myself. This was literally the first time in my life that I stood up for myself in front of an elderly person. I said, "What's your impression of me? What do you think of me? Nobody ever called me a thief. Are you trying to say I'm bad luck?" I was loud.

She didn't say anything. At thirteen, I didn't know how to sell. And it was so cold in there, I was getting sick. The sweatshirt didn't do anything. And it was starting to snow. I had no hat or gloves or coat. And on top of that, she called me a bad omen.

After she left, I stayed in the shop. There were no customers, so I turned off the light, locked the door, and went straight home.

When I got home, Mr. Bruce was there. Usually he'd be out during the daytime, but this time he was home.

"What are you doing here?" He started screaming at me. "I just had a call from Hagea."

I told him it was too cold in the store, and I had no clothes or nothing and that there was a blizzard outside. He told me he didn't care, that I had to do what he had told me to do, and that I had to get back to work. So I went back outside and kept working until late that night. When I got home Mr. Bruce was waiting for me, still mad. I told him that I couldn't work there anymore, that it was too cold and too hard and that I wanted to go to school. Mr. Bruce just ignored me. He went into his room and locked his door. I started thinking about how I was going to leave this house.

That's when the grudge started. The interaction between him and me wasn't like that before. Before, he would come home and ask, "How ya doin'?" After I quit my job, he didn't even look at my face.

I thought I would never go to school, because he was pissed at me. He was mad because I stopped working. So I did things to try to please him. I kept the house clean. He didn't ask me to clean the house, but I cleaned it to please him. I thought I should try to find another job. Meanwhile, I watched wrestling all day.

After winter, I think around March or April, I went outside. I still had the key to the apartment, so I could come and go whenever Mr. Bruce wasn't around. One day, I went outside and saw a girl stretching on the porch. She was going jogging. She said, "Do you live here?" I looked like a bushy person because I never went for a haircut and my hair was long and wild. That's probably why she asked, "Do you live here?"

"Yeah, I live here."

"Since when?"

"Oh, six or seven months."

"How come I've never seen you here?"

"I still live here. Just because you haven't seen me doesn't mean I don't live here." She said that I had an attitude.

J— breaks into a huge smile, giggling.

"What's your name?" she asked.

"What's *your* name?"

"I asked you first."

"Okay, ladies get to ask first. My name is J—."

"J—?"

"Noooo. J—! My name is J—." Her name was Nicole. She was sixteen or seventeen.

Nicole asked, "Where do you go to school?"

I said, "I don't go to school. I just came here six months ago. I don't go to school."

She said, "Do you work?"

"No, I don't work." I thought to myself that everybody must work in this country, because even Nicole asked me if I work.

"How old are you?"

I said, "You don't have to know my age or anything. How old are you? If you tell me how old you are, I won't lie to you, I swear."

"I'm about to turn seventeen."

"How soon?"

"Pretty soon."

"I'm thirteen years old."

"AND YOU DON'T GO TO SCHOOL?"

"Yeah." Then I asked her why she was so surprised.

"Because thirteen-year-olds do not stay home from school."

Nicole explained to me that she works and goes to school. I thought that must be the fashion here.

She asked me, "What do you do?"

I said, "I just sit around my house."

She said I should start jogging. Maybe I'd meet new friends. I started jogging, and Nicole became my first friend.

One day when we were jogging, I asked her if there was a way for me to get a job. And she asked again how old I was. I said I was going to be fourteen pretty soon, four months from now, in July. She was like, "And you really want a job?"

I said, "Yeah, I want to work and go to school like you."

"Yeah, but I didn't work when I was fourteen. I work now to save money for college."

"If you really want me to go back to school, then you'll help me get a job. Then I can go back to school." I thought I had to pay for school. When I arrived here, Mr. Bruce asked me to keep myself busy, like get a job, before I could go to school.

She was, like, "How? Why?"

"You don't want to know." I waved her off. I didn't know how to explain it to her.

Nicole told me about fast-food restaurants. She said she had a friend who's the manager at a McDonald's. She taught me how to read addresses, where the even side of the street is and where the odd side is. Nicole really taught me stuff.

She told me to go on Wednesday 'cause that's when the manager she knew was there. I didn't wait for Wednesday. I went right that very day.

"May I please speak to the manager?"

The worker there said, "Do you have a complaint or something?"

"No, I don't have a complaint. I just want to talk to the manager."

The manager came. "Are you guys hiring?"

"No, I don't think we're hiring."

"Are you sure? Because I was directed here."

"Okay, see that corner over there?" The manager pointed to a man sitting there. "Go see him. He's the owner of this McDonald's."

The owner asked me for my papers. "What papers? I don't have papers. I just need a job."

He was, like, "*You* need a job? How old are you?"

"I'm thirteen."

"You can't work here."

"Why?

"You have to go to school."

"People work and go to school. Why can't I work and go to school?"

"Because of your age. I'd be in trouble."

"Why would you be in trouble if you hired me? Is that a crime?"

"Yes," he said, "it *is* a crime." Meanwhile, I was thinking, what is this man saying? I mean, this country is not organized.

I explained to him, "At my age, I'm supposed to be in school . . ."

"Right."

"And both of us know that. But I wouldn't be able to go to school if I don't get this job."

"Because why?"

"Okay." I took a deep breath to give myself a minute to find the right words. "So right now I live with my uncle. I just came to this country with my uncle, and I don't have papers."

"So you're undocumented."

"What's undocumented?" That was the first time I heard the word *undocumented.*

He said, "Do you have a Social Security number or an I.D. card?"

I told him I had a passport but not with me. But I don't have an I.D.

The owner said, "Well, then, you're undocumented. Even if I wanted to hire you, I can't, because you don't have the necessary requirements for hiring. You're not eligible to be hired because of your age and the lack of papers."

"Is there any way you can help me? I can't go to school now. My uncle told me so." I was lying here, because my uncle never told me I couldn't go to school;

he said I would go to school after the summer. But I told the man I needed money to continue school. I had no choice but to lie. I would do anything to get back to school. I think he knew I was lying, but he saw my desperation.

"What are you talking about?"

I said, "I have an uncle who wants me to go to school, but then he realized if I finish high school, I wouldn't be able to go to college. So I need to work." I used Nicole's story because she's working to go to college

The owner looked at me and responded to my needs. He was a good man. He paid me personally out of his own pocket. And he told the manager to take good care of me because he was scared I could be bullied. I mopped the floor and washed the dishes.

The other employees weren't that nice to me. They teased me all the time. There was a movie called *Black Diamond*. They called me Black Diamond because of my dark skin. They asked dumb questions, like, "Did you harpoon animals?" Who uses a harpoon in the twenty-first century? They didn't understand we have supermarkets in Ghana just like here. But I said, "Yeah, I know how to do that." I just thought I'd say yes to everything.

One guy asked, "Do you see lions?"

Another guy made pushing sounds with his tongue to the bridge of his mouth: *clu, clu, clu, clu, clu, clu*. That's how he thought I talked. I thought these guys were very stupid.

The managers didn't know that the staff teased me, because I didn't want to complain. I pretended it didn't happen. I saw something missing in them. They didn't have much knowledge about what they said. Teasing or bullying a fellow human is irrational. They are ignorant and not looking at a human being as an individual.

The manager was always asking questions too. I wondered why he was so inquisitive. Too many questions! But I'm like that too. I always ask too many questions, so I couldn't complain.

I was too scared to tell Mr. Bruce I was working and making money, because he might take it from me. He left the house before I woke up, and he came home around ten or eleven. I took a shift between those time periods. I was making money and saving all of it. I still took care of cleaning his house.

In July, I asked Mr. Bruce again, When would I enroll in school? He didn't answer me. Mr. Bruce never physically abused me. He never really made money off me. He never had a fight with me. But he gave me no attention. Why did he bring me here? I don't know. Seriously. I didn't know. This is something I need to figure out.

I worked at McDonald's almost a year. And then something happened that changed my luck a third time.

Lucky Break Number Three

A smile fills J—'s face in anticipation of a dramatic change he's about to talk about. He takes a sip of water and stretches out on the couch.

Where was I? Oh, I was getting money from the job. One day the manager was going on vacation, and a new girl came to manage the store. I could tell from her voice and manner that she was from Ghana. When she saw me, she asked my name.

"I'm J—. I'm from Ghana."

"Me too. My name is Memmi. What are you doing here? The other manager asked me to take very good care of you. How do you like it here?"

I think the boss told her about me too. She asked so many questions. I felt like I was being interrogated. I answered her questions because I thought she was a nice person. I felt comfortable telling Memmi my story. Two weeks later, Memmi asked me what I was doing next Friday. That was my day off.

"Can you come here? I want to take you someplace."

I told her that I couldn't because Mr. Bruce was home Fridays. That Friday, though, Mr. Bruce went out. So I went out.

Memmi took me to a mosque. She asked, "Are you Muslim?"

"Yeah, I'm Muslim."

"Well, you're here to see someone."

"Who am I here to see?"

"Just shut up for a second. You ask too many questions," she told me.

She was laughing. We were standing at a door, and an older lady came out. Memmi said, "Granny, this is the boy I was talking about."

The lady said she was happy to meet me. She invited me to her house. She lived three blocks away from the mosque, but she didn't want us to walk, so we took a taxi. I was a little bit uncomfortable that Memmi told her grandmother things about me.

She told me her name was Humu. She was in her late sixties, not too tall, maybe five foot five. She was pretty, not many wrinkles on her face, and had only a little gray hair. She had a warm smile, a lovely, warm smile.

Humu started asking me many questions: Where do you live? How old are you? Do you go to school? Aren't you supposed to be in school by now?

"Yeah, but."

"Do you go to school at all?" She was impatient with my answers.

"No."

"Why?"

"I don't know." I didn't want to answer the questions because I didn't feel comfortable. She would not stop asking.

"Where are your parents?"

"They're in Ghana."

"You're from Ghana?"

"Yeah, I'm from Ghana."

"Well, let's speak Twi."

"I don't mind." When she asked me where my parents were, I explained that they were back in Ghana and that I lived with my uncle. I explained that my uncle was not my blood uncle, but like an old family friend of my parents.

"Well, why didn't he put you in school?"

"I don't know."

"Why do you say 'I don't know' to my questions?" She wouldn't let me escape my answers.

"Well, I don't have answers."

"Why were you brought here?"

"He told me he was bringing me here to go to school."

"Then why are you not in school?"

"He told me that school was already in session, and he had to wait to enroll me."

"That's not true. You can go to school right now. You can go to the Board of Education and register as a student."

"I didn't know that." I had been in the States for two years and no school. When I asked Mr. Bruce about school, he didn't say anything. He'd say, "Yeah, I want to enroll you, but I don't have time. I'll take you before school begins." He never did. I still don't know why he brought me here. Humu became quiet. Really quiet! I think she was shocked by what I told her.

"Can I talk to Mr. Bruce?"

Sitting at the edge of the sofa, J— jerks up. His body stiffens as he waves his hand back and forth.

"No, no, no, don't talk to him." I'm not a fearful person. Big people, tough-looking people, they don't scare me. But if you're very quiet, and I can't tell what sort of person you are, I'm fearful. Mr. Bruce never said a word. He'd shake his head. I didn't know what kind of reaction he would have to this lady. So I was uncomfortable. "No. No. I don't want to escalate stuff. All right?"

Humu backed down. She asked when I last spoke to my mom. I told her, "Not since the first day I came to this country," and she almost started to cry.

She asked if she could call my parents in Ghana, and I said, "Yes." For two years I couldn't call my parents, because I didn't know how to use a cell phone. I thought about asking Nicole or somebody from work. But then those thoughts literally disappeared from my head. I didn't know how or where to get a phone.

Humu told her granddaughter to go to the store and buy a calling card. I knew my mom's phone number but didn't know if she had changed it. She got the card and called my number.

"Mom?"

"Hello? Hello?"

"Mom?"

"Who's this calling me *mom*?"

"Mom, it's B——." That's what they called me at home, because they said I looked like my grandfather. His name was B——.

"B——!!!!!" And she started screaming, "B——! B——!"

Tears fall down J——'s cheeks as he re-creates the scene.

She was really happy. My mom gave the phone to my father, and I could hear her crying in the background. My parents said they kept calling and calling Mr. Bruce's cell, but the call always went to voice mail. Mr. Bruce never told me that my parents had tried to reach me. And there was no house phone, only his cell. That's why I couldn't talk to them.

> *J——'s lawyer says, "Bruce had a cell phone and probably heard J——'s parents calling on voice mail. Refusing to allow a child to have contact with family members is another tactic traffickers use to keep the child powerless."*

My father asked what happened, and I told him. I didn't tell them everything, but I told him I didn't go to school, I went to work. I said, "This lady here wants to speak to you."

Humu told them how I snuck out to go to work. She told them I wasn't going to school at all. She was using the calling card and didn't have much time.

My parents had never heard from Mr. Bruce, even though they were old friends. According to my parents, they helped him to come here. When he wanted to travel outside Ghana, my father gave him the money. That's why they assumed he'd be good to me.

Humu asked my parents what they wanted her to do. Should I stay in this country or go back to Ghana? If I stayed in this country, she said that she would take care of me. If I wanted to go back to Ghana, she would raise funds for me.

My mom took the phone and talked to me. "Why do you want to come to Ghana? Everything's messed up here. If this nice woman wants to take care of you, let that happen." She was crying. She put the phone on speaker. She said that she missed me but still wanted her son to have an education.

I needed time to think about this choice because it was a tough decision.

That was a dramatic day. Humu wanted to take me to my house and talk to Mr. Bruce.

"NOOOOO, I'M AFRAID!" I didn't tell her why I was afraid. To be honest, there was no reason to be afraid. I could go there and pack my stuff. Me leaving may even make him happy. But still, I was afraid.

I promised I would come back but maybe not right away. Humu gave me a hundred dollars. I had money saved up, but it was in my bag at home. She knew I had money, but she gave it to me anyway.

I went home, and Mr. Bruce was not there. I put everything in my bag. I only had the clothes that I came with two years ago, plus the sweatshirt. I threw my stuff in my bag and just wanted to get out. But Mr. Bruce came home and stayed there four days. I didn't go to work. I was scared to leave.

I knew Memmi was worried because she didn't see me anymore. I was thinking, maybe Mr. Bruce was a good person, trying to help out. He brought me over here and everything. Why did he bring me over here? He used his own money to bring me here. He even used his own money to get me a passport. Why?

I later found out that Mr. Bruce was a bad person. All along he was lying to me about everything. There was an agenda to all this. But what was it? Meanwhile, I stayed in the house. Saturday. Sunday. Monday. Tuesday.

Tuesday, Mr. Bruce went out, so I went running with Nicole. I was feeling pains in my leg because of my shoes. They were the same shoes my father bought for me when I left home two years earlier. Now they were too tight and falling apart. I stepped on a stone and started crying. Nicole didn't ask what's wrong. She must have been too embarrassed to ask. I told her my shoes were hurting, but I was thinking, I can't do this anymore. I came here to go to school, and I should go. I can't do this anymore!

I went home, took all my stuff, and went to McDonald's. The people at McDonald's had been so worried about me. I told them I was just thinking things through. I didn't want to get into trouble. Memmi took an early break and took me to her grandma's. We went to the Bronx, and that's where I live now, with Humu.

I never saw Nicole again. I never saw Mr. Bruce again. I wonder if he ever looked for me.

PART TWO: Grandma's House

When I arrived at her house, Humu embraced me. I think she was also worried about me. And she told me to call her Grandma.

This is a home to be in. It's a fun home. Friends can come by and everything. When Grandma cooks, she cooks as if she's expecting visitors. If anybody comes, there's always something to eat. My grandmother and her husband help support me. She works at a hotel as a housekeeper. He's a security guard at a construction site. I owe them a lot.

In early August, Grandma called 311 and asked when school began. When she realized there was not much time, she called my parents in Ghana to get my birth certificate, transcripts, and immunization card. She sent them money so that they could mail the documents express. She wanted me to start school on time.

Now I wonder how Mr. Bruce could have promised to put me in school if he didn't have my transcripts. That's one of the questions I would like answered.

Every Sunday Grandma called my parents. She knew that my parents didn't have money. She also knew that the school didn't want to give them my transcripts because of my father's old debt. She gave them money to pay for my school fees and the transcripts. She didn't want me to spend my money that I saved from working at McDonald's. Grandma did in a few weeks what Mr. Bruce would never do.

Grandma got all the necessary transcripts. She got the authorization from my parents to do things on my behalf. Then she took me to a school, only five minutes from the house, where I was placed in the eleventh grade.

Schoolboy

Going to school was great but weird. I didn't make animal noises or act goofy, because I didn't feel comfortable yet. I sat in class quietly and did my work. Everyone at school liked me. I don't know, maybe it's my style. I made four special friends, and everywhere I go, I mention their names: Roshoun. Jeremy. David. D——.

D— was a senior. When I got to the school, the counselor said, "You have to meet D—. He's a very good student." He's from Jamaica.

We studied in a classroom during lunch. That's how we became friends. I liked being with D— because I like being around people who are more mature. He was always top of the class. I couldn't beat him. At one point I thought, I don't like this guy. He beats me. He was always on the honor roll. His grade point average was a hundred. Who gets 100 percent? He was too clever. I only got 88 percent.

Once D— graduated, I became the top student. When soccer season started, I was made captain. Grandma worried about me because I was undocumented. She said, "Be careful when you go out to play soccer. Don't get in trouble. You will get deported." She made it clear to me that if something happened, even if I was innocent, I could get deported. I really loved her for worrying about me, for caring about me.

I couldn't tell my friends that I was undocumented. The only people who knew were my counselor and D—. Because I was undocumented and wasn't eligible for DACA, I couldn't travel out of the country. My grandmother and her husband went to Ghana to visit my parents. They saw my big sister graduate from secondary school. My grandma and her husband are part of our family.

I was always pretty shy around girls, except my sisters, of course. In my senior year I had my first relationship with a girl. She was smart and very pretty. She was Hispanic. She was born here and everything. We went out alone and sometimes with friends. She was the first person I ever kissed. She liked me partly because she thought I was intelligent. We applied to every college together. But I didn't want to go to the school she chose, so she broke up with me.

"How to Go to College and Other Immigration Issues"

At the end of my junior year, I had not thought about applying to college. I had taken and passed all my Regents [college entrance exams]. My lowest score was eighty-two. The teachers and counselors were surprised. I wasn't surprised. School was easy because it was where I wanted to be.

"I couldn't tell my friends that I was undocumented."

D— gave me advice about how to apply to colleges. I wrote the advice on a sticky note and pasted it on my computer. I wrote, "How to go to college and other immigration issues."

The summer of 2013, I searched Google to find nonprofit organizations that help people with education issues. Nothing came up. Then I tried "nonprofit organizations for citizens who need help." Nothing came up. "Nonprofit organizations for illegal aliens." Aha! I got a list from the U.K. and Australia. No, that's not what I wanted. The sixth day of searching, I typed "nongovernmental organizations for undocumented students who need help." And a bunch of organizations came up. But most were not for my needs.

On page twenty-six, I found a group called Atlas. There was a YouTube video, and I clicked on it. Lauren, the director of the organization, was explaining how to apply for immigration relief and things like that. She said that if you don't have money for a lawyer, Atlas could help. I thought, these are good people.

I clicked on another page and found the address, Thirty-Fourth Street. But I didn't see it was in Brooklyn. I wrote down the address and took the train to Manhattan. But there was no building at the address on my paper.

I tried calling, but only a machine was on. Then I went to the train station and asked, "Is this the only Thirty-Fourth Street?"

I hadn't written *Brooklyn,* but I had the zip code. The man in the booth said I had to take a D train to Brooklyn. But I didn't have enough money on my MetroCard to add a ride.

Lucky Break Number Four

The man in the booth wrote a note on the paper so I could go and come home for free. That was another lucky break. It took me six to seven hours to finally get to the office. When I arrived, Lauren was on break. I was anxious 'cause I wanted to go to college so badly. I worried that my illegal status would keep me out of school. I met Suzy and Mohammad in the office. They said, "Just relax. We've got you. Relax," and they gave me water.

Lauren came in, and my life changed again. When I told Lauren my story, she said, "This is trafficking." I knew about trafficking from movies and stuff, but I didn't know that I was trafficked. I learned that I was considered trafficked except for two things: Mr. Bruce didn't adopt me, and he wasn't selling me for sex. But the fact that he pushed me to work and kept me in the house for a long time met the definition.

Lauren filed a T visa, for victims of trafficking. T visas expire in four years, but after the third year, I can file for a green card. With a T visa, I can bring my siblings and my family to visit me if I feel lonely.

I was given a letter from the Bureau of Homeland Security, a temporary approval letter saying that my application was pending. It was with this letter that I got my Social Security number and federal financial aid for college. In the meantime, if I needed any help — insurance or anything — Atlas would work to get it for me.

It took almost eight months to get my T visa. When Lauren called to tell me, we were both excited. Lauren is like my American mom. She makes sure that I'm on track with everything. She doesn't take no for an answer. She's funny, just like my mom. I'm lucky to know Lauren. I also have a lawyer, Becky. Becky is my cheerleader. She says I can do anything. "You can do this!" With Lauren and Becky in my life, my family is growing.

J— is currently a student at a college in upstate New York, majoring in accounting with a minor in computer science.

Portrait: T—

CHAPTER SEVEN

THE AMERICAN DREAM
IS SO POWERFUL
T——

T—— was born in Manu, Independent Samoa. She was twelve when her father told her that their family was going to leave their paradise island and move to America. They traveled as a family on her father's visa.

There are seven kids in our family, five boys and two girls. I'm in the middle, the oldest sister. Life was easy. At least I think it was easy. We played outside on the beach and in a big old front yard. We did chores, like pick up the fallen breadfruit leaves in the front yard and gather coconuts, taro, and bananas for dinner from the plantation. The plantation was the village's land. You just picked what you needed. Nowadays a family owns the plantation, so you have to ask.

We usually ate fish or chicken. We would just fish in the ocean or look around for the little chickens running around the backyard. There was one village store where we would buy meat for dinner, but it was very expensive.

People in our village brought our family food because of my dad's position. My dad was the pastor, and in Samoan culture, the pastor gets the most respect. We were very proud of our dad. The villagers gave us children a lot of respect too because we were the pastor's children. But then again, we had to be extra good because we were the pastor's children. We couldn't be too loud. We had to mind our manners. We had to serve food to the villagers when they had meetings at church.

In Samoa, most of our culture revolves around respect. You respect your parents. You respect your elders. You respect your heritage. You respect your church. You respect each other.

For example, everyone respected our grandma, our father's mother. She was big and she was old. When she talked to us, she was a get-to-the-point kind of person. She'd just sit in her chair while the grandkids ran around her. She'd yell at us to do this and do that. She couldn't walk. And she wasn't a very affectionate person.

Grandma's house was one big, open room. Bean curtains were hung for privacy. She didn't have an oven. We made a fire outside in a pit filled with dried coconut leaves. That's where we cooked our food.

Sharing Gifts

On Saturdays, we went with our dad when he made his rounds to the congregation's families. He'd pray for them and ask how they were doing. We all prayed with them. We wore *puletasi,* a two-piece wardrobe — a sarong and a top that was hand-sewn. Sometimes I liked going, but not all the time. My dad got up way too early.

When there was a wedding or a funeral, my dad would be given part of a cow as a gift. They gave him, like, a whole leg, because he led the event. Dad always shared his gifts with my grandma, aunts, and uncles.

My dad wore an *ielava,* a wraparound for men, and a dress-up shirt. He would get his clothes from my aunt overseas because material is too expensive in Samoa. His suits — he would wear a suit on Sundays — were from relatives in California or my aunt in New Zealand. My mom made our other clothes.

My father wasn't really a stern man. He was a proper man who was very mindful of his flock. We tried to obey him, because we respected and loved him. My mom was always with my dad. She helped the women and the children. She led classes, like sewing, Sunday school, and a youth fellowship program. At home she cooked and cleaned up after us.

My dad's salary came from church tithing. We did pay for our schooling, but it wasn't very expensive. We had a TV, but no one watched it. We had a car but only used it to visit Grandma. We walked to school. Our village was crime free. We knew everyone.

The Calling

My dad was a minister of the Congregational Christian Church of Samoa, also known as CCCS. When I was twelve years old, an independent church different from ours called upon my dad to move to Los Angeles and help build a church. Many Samoans lived in Los Angeles and prayed in a rented church.

I was excited and sad about moving to America. It was a bittersweet moment. "Yay, I'm going to America!" I told my friends.

Then: "Oh, my God, we're going to go to America?"

"Are you coming back? Are you coming back?" My friends couldn't believe I was leaving them.

"Yeah, we'll come back and visit." We still had my grandma there. I was only twelve years old at the time and had not traveled beyond my grandmother's village, which was twenty-five miles from our house.

It was such a weird time for me. Samoa was all I had ever known my whole life, and now we were going on a big plane and leaving all our family and friends. We moved all our stuff from the church housing to my grandmother's house.

We said a million good-byes to our grandmother. That was really hard. We had so many lectures from her. "Go to school. Come back home to get married. Make sure you call me once a week. Write letters. Take care of your parents. Set good examples for the church kids to follow."

Yes. Yes. Yes. Yes. Yes. Yes.

Los Angeles, California

We flew to Los Angeles in an airplane that was big and cold and scary. All of us were scared throughout the fourteen-hour flight.

Then, when we arrived at the airport — oh, my God — the airport was huge. HUGE. My little brothers started crying. They were scared because there were so many things moving around — steps, baggage, even food behind glass cases — oh, so many things.

A man in a van picked us up and drove onto the freeway. That was crazy. I had never seen so many cars in my life. I couldn't believe how big this America was.

We were taken to our new house. It had a kitchen, a bathroom, and a bathtub. Our first bath in a bathtub was awesome. We had bubbles. We called it our swimming pool. Then we got to go to a real swimming pool, and that was even more exciting. Before we had an ocean to swim in, but a swimming pool? Never. It was awesome.

The church provided us with a car, but my dad didn't have a U.S. license. Other people drove us, or we took the bus, or we walked. The church paid for our house. We had to pay for everything else — food, clothing, and so on. My parents' only income was from the church, which was, like, a thousand a month for seven kids. Back home I didn't know anything about money. Then I came here, and, oh, my God, there were so many *things* to buy. Cool things. I became a big nagger. I wanted this and I wanted that. And I needed this and I needed that. My parents were not able to afford all the things we wanted. They tried. We were able to get some stuff. That's when I realized, wow, living in America is harder than I thought.

At first I was happier in Samoa than in L.A. In Samoa, there were not so many things to worry about. We never thought about money, and now we thought about it all the time. In Samoa, we just picked our food. Now we bought our food. In Samoa, we played outside, and it was safe. Here we played mostly inside because my parents thought it wasn't safe outside. We were exposed to movies, television, and crime.

The church wasn't a big church; it was medium size. People came back and forth as they moved between Samoa and the States. There was always money drama. We had to have many fundraisers — dances and potluck dinners — for the new church.

I questioned our living here. "Why are we here, Dad? Back home everything is free. And the church is less stressful. People come and go all the time here."

"You'll learn when you get older. It's better for you here."

We were here on a visitor visa, but my parents wanted something more permanent. The church was filing for our papers, but we had to pay lawyers lots of money so that they could deal with immigration.

A new problem arose. The main church in Samoa, the CCCS, informed T—'s father that he was not ordained to preach in an independent church. The CCCS invited her father's new church to join them; they wanted to remain independent.

My father stopped working as an ordained minister in L.A. He became unemployed. We moved into my aunt's five-bedroom home. It sounds like a big house, but it was small considering who already lived there: my dad's brother, wife, their three kids; dad's sister, her husband, their son; and dad's older sister and her partner.

When I turned fifteen, my grandmother passed away. We went back to Samoa for the funeral and stayed there for ten months. Then one of my aunts, my dad's sister, passed away in Los Angeles. We returned for her funeral with tourist visas. When the visas ran out, we stayed in L.A. My dad thought it would be better for us to go to school here and have a good future and education than to live back home. Five of us siblings stayed in L.A., and the two older boys went to live with our uncle in New Zealand.

We enrolled in public school because we couldn't afford to send everyone to private school. It was hard to get into school here. It required a lot of paperwork. By this time, we no longer had legal papers. My brothers, sisters, and I did not know about this, though. My parents thought that we should concentrate on school and not worry about such things. I wish that we had talked about our status, but we didn't. We just didn't talk about it. Once, when we went to a lawyer's office, the subject came up. "Why are we here?" I asked my parents.

"Oh, we have to fix something."

"Fix what?"

"A thing so that we can get jobs."

I think that's the only time we'd ever talked about it. It's still a very hard topic in our family. It stressed my parents so much, they just don't want to think about it.

As I got older, I became more American. I wanted to drive. I wanted to travel. I wanted to go here and there with my friends. We couldn't afford it.

I had friends from school but didn't go out with them much. We were usually at church activities. When I did go out, my parents were okay about it so long as they knew whom we were with. Sometimes my dad or mom wanted to go with us. That was definitely not cool. Even when I was in high school, my dad would not let me go to the movies with friends unless one of them went with us. He would make my older brother come along with us. It was humiliating.

"You can trust us," I'd complain.

"Well, just go to the movies. Don't go wandering off." He was afraid that someone would kidnap us, or that we would go someplace nasty, or that we would steal something.

Yeah, steal. Do you believe it? Dad actually said, "Maybe you will go to a store, see something you want, and steal it." He was so afraid that we would get into trouble.

The Field Trip

I didn't know that I was undocumented until I was graduating from high school. We were going to take a field trip to Catalina Island. I didn't understand why I couldn't go. The school needed some kind of American I.D. I didn't have anything. My parents were too scared to give them my passport. And then they told me why: they were afraid that it would tell everyone that I didn't have my papers, and the kids would make fun of me, and I'd probably get talked about. They were trying to protect me. I ended up not going on my senior trip to Catalina Island.

I tried to get some kind of identification because I wanted an after-school job. I looked online for something, but they always asked for a Social Security number. I didn't have one, so I couldn't work. My cousin was working in a warehouse. They were paying under the table. I worked with her, and they were able to pay me cash. My dad was not happy about this.

I gave my name but not my address, because I thought that my dad would kill me. I worked as a packager in the warehouse. They paid me seven dollars an hour. It was less than minimum wage, but I took it because we needed the money. At least I could help my parents by contributing something. I worked there about eight months, right after school. The owner of the warehouse said he would sponsor me for my papers and stuff if I wanted to work full-time. But I couldn't drop out of school. That would hurt my parents.

That's about the time I lost my focus. I thought, why am I going to high school? Why should I go to college? I can't even get a job. What can I do with a degree? Whatever. It was hard watching my parents try so hard to find ways to get money to pay for our education.

My parents wanted to do things legally. The plan was to send me back home and then apply for a student visa so that I could return and go to school as an international student — which is what I legally was. But at this point we didn't have enough money for a plane ticket. And going to college as a full-time international student is much more expensive than a regular American student. We were stuck.

Where were we going to get so much money? My brother was planning to go to college too. We went to a community college, but we couldn't afford going as full-time students. We tried to apply for financial aid. We weren't eligible. We were on our own. You might be wondering why we gave up our easy life in Samoa to do this. 'Cause this is America! The American dream is very powerful. For us to go to school, get a good education, make a career, and build a family here is worth the troubles.

When I was applying for college, and the tuition thing came up, I could see the stress in my parents' eyes. We paid all our bills in cash. I watched as my mother held back on things for herself in order to pay for college. It made me thankful but sad.

I wasn't eager to go to college, because my parents were struggling. But they pushed me. I'm glad they did.

I missed a whole semester of college, just trying to get into one. I had to go through the dean and administration to get into the college that I went to. That's because the college needed two forms of U.S.-issued government I.D.s, which I didn't have. I had to go through lawyers and church officers in order to prove I had been in the U.S. for my father's occupation. The letters took forever.

The tuition was really high because we had to pay the international school fees. My mother started doing housekeeping work to help pay for my brother's and my college. She saved every penny so that we could finish college. We did get into the colleges of our choice, but we couldn't afford the huge tuition costs. That's why we went to a community college instead. I studied business.

Then my dad got sick.

Dad

Early one morning, around four a.m., I heard a thump in front of my sister's and my bedroom. It was my father. He had fainted. My mother came running from their bedroom. She shook him, and he immediately woke up. Although he insisted that he was fine, I could see the uncertainty in his eyes. Mom begged him to go to the hospital, but he refused. Two days later, the same thing happened. Out of nowhere he fell. Again, he said that he was okay. After the third fall, he finally gave in and went with Mom to the hospital to see what was wrong. We were all worried, so worried. Mom and Dad were at the hospital for almost a whole day. That's when I knew something really bad was happening. Mom and Dad gathered us around to say the evening prayer like we always did. It was like nothing had happened. But we all knew something serious was going to change our lives.

Two weeks later, coming home from church, my mom said that they had something to tell us. It was the longest drive of my entire life. Once we were home, though, all she said was that Dad was very sick and that we needed to be good and not give him a hard time. She never mentioned the word *cancer*. The only way we found out about it was when my brother answered a call from the hospital to schedule his chemotherapy appointment. My brother asked, "Why does my father need chemotherapy? What does he have?"

"He has stage-four lung cancer."

There couldn't have been a worse possible way for us to find this out. My brother called and told me. I never cried. I just felt so much love for my father. I felt so sad for my mother, wondering why she had to carry such a burden alone. My heart ached for my siblings. All I could think of was Dad's going to die soon. Due to the sickness, so much had changed tremendously in such a short time. We were never angry that our parents didn't tell us it was cancer. I mean, how could we be?

Time went on, and we all were there for Dad. I stopped going to school and stayed home to help my mom take care of Dad. I never returned. People from the church that we attended brought us food.

We got to the point where we were doing small things for him, like trying to get him to drink or eat. My father passed away on a gloomy Monday morning. The cancer had reached his brain, and his body could not take it anymore. It was the worst day of all our lives.

"It feels good to fight for the rights of immigrants."

DACA

Eight months later, DACA came out, and we were able to get jobs to help keep the family stable. As soon as I got my Social Security number, I applied everywhere for a job. I was so happy that I could put money toward my Social Security.

I went to lots of interviews. I chose a job at a hotel because I thought it was a place where I could work my way up and have a real career. I started in housekeeping, cleaning rooms. Two and a half months later, I was put on the front desk. I worked my butt off. It was my first real job in America, and I really enjoyed it. I'm now an assistant general manager at a hotel and making a good salary.

Lots of people in my church are immigrants. Like my family, they don't want people to know their status. I'm trying to change that. I say to them, "How are we going to ever have our voices heard if we don't come out of the shadows?" There are not many Pacific Islanders out there protesting or rallying. It's mostly Asians and Hispanics who are the activists. But there are so many of us living here, you wouldn't believe it. We are just not active.

Recently, I went to a public protest. It felt good to get my voice out there. It feels good to fight for the rights of immigrants. My mom almost killed me. She said, "Yes, your voice should be heard. But someone may shoot you." My mom watches too much TV.

Portrait: G—

CHAPTER EIGHT

GO BIG OR GO HOME
G——

In a stylish cafe in Arizona, eighteen-year-old G—— flashes a silver smile and talks about his life in America. Like P—— and C——, he came from Mexico. But he did not walk to the United States. He and his family packed up their belongings and drove across the border with visitor visas. Once the visas expired, they moved into the shadows.

When I say good morning to my parents, I'm never sure that I will be able to say good night to them. I'm afraid to go to school, because it could be the last time I see them for a while. My dad's got to go to work. He's got to drive to get there. Because he does not have a U.S. license, if a police officer pulls him over, he could end up in jail. Once he's in jail, he could go through deportation proceedings. It's happened to some of my friends — their parents get deported, and they are left alone.

I want to be able to give my parents what they've given to me — but ten times more. All my opportunities would not be possible had we stayed in Mexico. If we had stayed in Mexico, like most of my family, I'd be working at a shoe factory, trying to make enough to put food on the table.

The National Anthem

I was born in León, Mexico, but I've mostly lived in the U.S. I came here when I was five. I started first grade here. I sometimes feel like I've forgotten some of my Spanish. I know the American national anthem. I don't know the Mexican anthem. Basically my whole life has been as an American. I feel American, but I don't have the documentation to prove it. We're good people. We pay our taxes. We have no criminal record. We would like to legalize our status, but the process is so long. Because of the long waiting line, our attorney said it would take ten to fifteen years if we did it through our family members who are citizens.

When we lived in Mexico, we used to visit our U.S. family all the time. We all had visitor visas. My older brother who is closest to me in age saw how much our cousins were learning and wanted to finish high school here. He and my dad came first and lived with our U.S. family. The rest of the family followed a year or two later on what is called a visa overstay.

The decision to emigrate was made like any other: at the kitchen table. My parents talked about the pros and cons.

The cons were that my dad would lose his job. He had a very good job, and could afford to pay for visas for us to visit the U.S. The rest of our family wasn't as fortunate. They lived mostly from paycheck to paycheck.

Everything we had in Mexico would be pretty much gone. We'd leave behind my grandparents, my aunt, my uncle, and my cousins. The pros were that eventually we'd be able to send money to our family left behind, because the U.S. dollar had more value than the Mexican peso. Also, we kids would get a better education, and there was less fear of violence. My family went for the pros.

The Arrival

We drove through the port of entry in Douglas, Arizona, as we usually did. But this time we never went back. I'm eighteen now. That was thirteen years ago.

I remember coming through the port of entry that last time. My parents told me if police asked me why we were coming, I should say, "We're going to visit our family." We brought lots of clothes with us. We told the border police we were going to do a yard sale over here with our family. They believed us. I guess it was easier back then. My two older brothers were with me at the time, and my parents, of course. It was simple. The officer gave me a lollipop.

My first experience with the language barrier was my first day of school. I had to take the bus home. The bus driver asked me where I lived, and I didn't know what she meant, because she asked in English. I broke down and cried. I was crying until some girl I had never met came over and translated for me. She grabbed my hand and sat next to me the whole time. She helped me calm down and explained what was going on.

When I got home, I didn't want to go back to school. I was scared. I was afraid to go on the bus. My teacher was very friendly, and so were the other students. My teacher knew Spanish.

I learned English really fast. By the third grade I was speaking clearly. I still had a little accent, but I was able to ask questions and hold a conversation.

During the first couple of years, we lived at my aunt's house. She's my dad's sister. We went to yard sales. It was the easiest way to get clothes cheap. We even got furniture at yard sales. Our first apartment had a small

TV, a couch, and dishes. My uncle was a handyman who made furniture. He made our beds.

My father's first job was as a landscaper. It was menial labor. He did that for three years. If it rained, he didn't work that day. It wasn't stable employment. Then my uncle got him a job where he works now. Even though he couldn't put a Social Security number on his application, they still hired him. He's a machinist. It's precision work, where he works with designers making precision parts used in machinery. He's been working in the same place for twelve years now.

When I Was Twelve

"Mom, can we get my I.D.?"

"What I.D. are you talking about?"

"The one from here, from Arizona, with my picture. All my friends have it."

She stood quiet for a little bit and then looked at me. "We can't get one of those, because you're not from here."

I knew I wasn't from here. I just didn't know there had to be documentation.

"You have to have some papers to prove that you're from here."

"What do you mean? I *am* here!" I was around eleven or twelve and didn't understand what she meant.

She went into more depth. "You're not a resident or a citizen." Once she told me that, the rest of the walk home was quiet. I started wondering what that meant. I read more about politics. I read what it meant to be a resident. I read what it meant to be a citizen. And I read about the category I was in: an undocumented immigrant.

It messed with my head. My Latino friends, who are all USA-American citizens, would invite me to visit their families in Nogales on the Mexico side. I had to say no. And I could not tell them why I couldn't go.

Only one of my close Latino friends knows my situation. I'm still afraid that when they find out, they may look at me differently. Unfortunately, when some people get their documents, they think they are better than others. That's something I'm going to have to face. I think this book is a good way to come out of the shadows. Go big or go home! That's my motto. It'll be interesting to see how my friends respond when they read this. Right now I'm in limbo.

My one friend who knows keeps very quiet about it. When our group makes comments or jokes about undocumented immigrants, he'll give me a look. We'll make eye contact and look away. For example, my friends will see a cop and start messing around. "Oh, watch out," they say, laughing. "We are going to be deported." I know they are just playing. But in the back of my head I'm thinking, "I *could* be deported."

A Latino Boy Scout

Eagle Scout! I'm an Eagle Scout now. Usually Latinos like me don't join things like the Boy Scouts, but I did. One day, my dad and I went to the convention center, where there was a Scout-recruiting booth. The lady behind the table spoke Spanish, so we had a connection. I became a Cub Scout. This was before I found out I was undocumented. Yes, that's right. I had no idea that I was undocumented.

Once I moved up and became a Boy Scout, I kind of got teased by some of my Latino friends. None of them were Boy Scouts. It wasn't a big deal. It was friendly teasing.

I tried to go to every Scouting event. We lived about two or three miles from the place where they held their meetings. My mom and I walked because we didn't have a car. I went higher and higher in rank and badges. The Scout leader was my first real mentor. He taught me how to follow the Scout oath. He taught me that the oath wasn't just something to say; it was something to live by.

A few years later, another Scoutmaster was one of the few people who knew about my situation. His sons became my close friends. It was weird coming out to him, because he's a Republican. I'm on the opposite side. There were times when we would argue about immigration reform. It got kind of awkward. We argued about President Obama's decision to give students Deferred Action, DACA. We argued about politics. I told him that politicians don't look at the type of person you are or what you've done. They say, "If a small group messed up, you all have to suffer the consequences." But for some reason, my Scoutmaster has always been there for me. He helps me. He's offered to give me a recommendation if ever I need one. He's even offered to get me a job at the company where he works. He's taken me along on a family trip to California. It shows that once you get to know someone, the paper is just paper. We put aside our political differences and deal with each other as individuals.

When I was ten, my parents kept me home from school because of some kind of ceremony. My parents would never let me miss school. Something fishy was going on, but what was it?

I was given a Young American Award for "exceptional leadership" in my Scout pack. It's kind of ironic because I'm not even American. The thing is, if you're born in North or South America, you're American. But you're not USA American.

My parents were so proud. I felt weird because I was the only Latino getting an award. Everyone else was white.

Phone Call

About five years ago, when I was thirteen, my oldest brother was caught with marijuana. He was in jail for a year before he was deported back to Mexico. My parents were afraid that they would get arrested if they visited him. I didn't have DACA yet, so I couldn't go either.

Once he was sent back to Mexico, he turned his life around. He got a job as a construction worker and met a girl who he planned to marry.

On a regular, normal Sunday morning, we went to the grocery store. My mom's sister had just come to visit, and we wanted to make a nice meal. They hadn't seen each other for eight years.

While we were in the store, my dad got a phone call from my other brother, who had stayed home that day. At first, I saw my father bow his head. Then he said to me, "We need to go home." I knew something big was wrong. We started going back toward the car. My mom kept saying, "What's going on? Why won't you guys tell me?"

I called my brother from the car. He broke down crying, saying, "They killed our brother!"

I was able to keep quiet because I knew that my mom would get hysterical. We needed to be home before we told her. When we got home my mom ran into my brother's and my room. We live in a three-bedroom house, but the family from out of town was using one room, and my brother and I were sharing the other room.

My mom saw my brother crying. She thought about the options: "Is he in jail . . . was he kidnapped . . . is he hurt?" The last option was "Did they kill him?" My brother bowed his head down. My mom completely broke down.

About a week earlier, we had tried to call my brother on his cell phone and got no response. We've since learned that he and two other guys were taking a taxi home from work. The driver of the taxi owed the cartels money, or something like that. The killers stopped the taxi. They killed the driver first. In order to leave no witnesses, they killed the three passengers, one of whom was my brother. He was in the wrong place at the wrong time.

We found out that he was still alive after they first shot him. I guess he was trying to play dead and he moved a little bit, and they shot him again in the head.

My uncle said that the family he lived with had a funeral for him. It was a closed casket. We weren't able to do anything. We couldn't go back to claim the body. My uncle, who is a U.S. citizen, went to Mexico and brought back his ashes.

Now there's a piece of us missing from our family. Every day I feel that piece missing. When asked if I have any brothers and sisters, I say, "I had two brothers and now I'm left with one."

I held back my feelings for two weeks. I thought that I had to be brave for my mom. One night, I stepped outside and started crying. My brother came out and put his arms around me. And then my mom came and hugged both of us. After that, we talked about it as a united family.

At the next Boy Scout meeting, the leader took me aside and said that they had heard what happened. He said, "This is a rock in the road that you must pass. We're here for you."

By this time, it was as if I lived in two different worlds. When I was at the Scout meetings, I was confident; I knew what I was doing. When I was at school, I was very hesitant; I wasn't sure what I was doing. I didn't trust my classmates enough to say that I was undocumented. It's ironic, because the kids in the Scouts were white, and the kids at school were like me.

When a death this close hits you, things change. I knew that I had to change. I could no longer stay in a shell in school. I had to take risks. I thought, well, I only live once, and there are things I have to do. I started to develop close friendships at school as well as in the Scouts. Now I have best friends for life in both places.

I take more risks. I'm out there. Back then, I probably would have been too shy to talk about this. This is another risk I'm taking. I want to share my story.

Student Reporter

In middle school I read a kids' newspaper. There was an ad that said, "Become a student reporter." I wrote some stories and submitted them. I never found out if they were actually printed. The truth is, I didn't think much about it until I got to high school.

In high school I started writing for the school newspaper. Then I went to a workshop held by a media group, and I won third place in a story-writing contest. That's when I thought, I like this, and I'm good at it to some extent. My dream to become a journalist began. It's what I want to do for the rest of my life.

I became a student television producer for a show we put on at my high school. I was the producer for *Current Events*. I would sum up current events to the student body. We tried to do a little bit of everything: politics, sports, personal stories, and entertainment.

My parents understood that I was growing up and needed more independence. But my mom still waited up for me to come home at night. Like a classic Latina mom, she worries. She cooks. She gives me advice and support. I have it easier than my older brothers did. I know that for sure. When we arrived here, my mom wasn't used to American ways. She was stricter with my brothers. She called them little devils, and they were. They would go out and not come home till morning. It drove her crazy. I was the calm one. I was a good kid who studied hard. But still, she's very cautious because of the experiences she had in the past with my brothers.

June 15, 2012

President Obama announced an executive action to help undocumented students, DACA. I was at home, watching the announcement on TV. It was like a rock was taken off my shoulders. This was such a great opportunity for me. I would have the possibility to grow and do more things. When the application was released, my brother and I immediately signed up.

The application asked for my whole name and my parents' names and our address. We were hesitant at first about giving out all that personal information on an immigration application, because we didn't know if it was a trick to get personal information. But my parents encouraged us. They wanted a future for my brother and me. We filled it out with the help of an attorney because we were still scared about what could happen.

It was really cool when my brother's and my DACA cards came in the mail. To celebrate, we went out to eat. We had hamburgers. We were happy and excited about the new opportunities. But there was one glitch. The same day that President Obama gave us DACA, then-governor of Arizona Jan Brewer signed an executive order. It prohibited anyone who received Deferred Action through the president's action from getting state benefits, including driver's licenses. It felt like being punched in the face. We won the battle getting some type of legal status, and then, from behind, we got hit with a cheap shot we weren't expecting. When the governor did that, I thought, I can work, but how am I going to get to work? If I drive without a license, I'm breaking the law. It was a no-win situation.

It's hard to knowingly break a law of the country you want to be part of. We broke a law by letting our visas expire. And now I had to break a law again. There was no way I was going to miss school. I needed a driver's license to get an education. I needed a license to drive to work and help my family. So I was helping the family, but I was also breaking the law. It was tough living with that.

Mr. G—— Goes to Washington

Last year, when I was a senior in high school, my teacher asked me to leave the classroom. We went into another room that was empty but for a second teacher. I thought I was in big trouble. What had I done? They had such funny smiles on their faces. Finally they shouted, "YOU'RE GOING TO WASHINGTON!"

I couldn't believe what I was hearing. I jumped and screamed. Earlier in the year my teacher had nominated me to be part of a special program for national student reporting. I was selected to be one of eleven in the country — and the only Latino — to go to Washington, to the White House, and to interview a colonel in the army. I felt like I was dreaming. I walked out of that class as happy as could be.

The only bad part was I couldn't tell my friends why I was so happy until the press release was revealed. I had to hold it in for about a week. The other students would look at me weird because I couldn't stop smiling.

My parents worried about me going to Washington alone, but I convinced them it would be okay. My DACA card could be used as an authorization at the airport. It was the first time I had ever gone on an airplane. It was scary, I'm not going to lie — I was scared.

When I gave my authorization card to the guard at the gate, he gave me a weird look. Everyone else had a state I.D. or driver's license. But he let me pass through the gate.

Once on the plane, I was more nervous. We took off, and I felt strange pressure in my ears. Then my ears popped. I didn't know that would happen. I sat in my seat the whole time, looking out the window. I wish I had known there was a bathroom on the plane.

Four days in D.C., all expenses paid! Pretty cool! I was like a little kid again, curious about everything. Sometimes I thought I was dreaming. It had never crossed my mind that I would get to see our nation's capital.

"YOU'RE GOING TO WASHINGTON!"

I felt blessed. I felt grateful to my parents because they made the decision that gave me this opportunity. Let me tell you, it was a really good feeling.

At the airport a cab picked me up and took me to a hotel at the National Harbor in Maryland. Compared to Arizona, it was very green and a little humid. I took pictures of all the buildings. They looked so old to me, ancient. Then I saw the Washington Monument, and the trip became real.

There were ten others in our group, from all across the country. I was nervous because I was the only one from Arizona. We had a meet-and-greet the first night. I sat there the first half hour, just looking around. Finally I went to talk to one of the other students, who was from Hawaii. A female. We started talking about our flights, and I got out of my shell.

The days that followed were amazing. Amazing! We went to the White House. I didn't meet the president, but I met his two dogs. It was cool, because you see them on the news. They were outside, doing their business. I did get to pet one of them. Really cool! They were very friendly. Then we got a tour of the White House. Standing where the president stands to deliver a speech is just an astonishing experience. Our group then interviewed a colonel in the United States Army. It was amazing that someone so high up on the chain of command would take time to meet eleven high-school journalists.

There was a set topic. It was about the Joining Forces initiative. My question to him was "How do you plan on making the Joining Forces initiative accessible to everybody?" He gave me his answer, but I couldn't focus while he was talking, because I couldn't believe I was there. Wow! A colonel of the United States Army answering *my* question!

Another important part of the trip was meeting other teens who were interested in becoming journalists. We've become a little network. We are all on Facebook together.

After

I finished my first semester of college at a community college. My grade point average was 4.0. Good grades are a must! If I don't do well, who knows what can happen, right? It's pressure. If I mess up, I feel that I will let down the entire family. Studying isn't that difficult, because I enjoy what I'm learning. Besides, I like to look at the positive side of everything. In my view, homework is a learning skill that I can use in the future — like having to meet deadlines.

I'd love to transfer to the Cronkite School at Arizona State University to study journalism. Unfortunately, at this time, Arizona State does not offer in-state tuition to DACA students. Although I tutor in a local high school, I don't make enough for college tuition. Besides, I'm still paying off my dental braces.

Did I mention the braces? I decided I needed them. As a journalist I need to have a good physical appearance, so there are certain things I have to do. I told my parents I didn't want them to pay for my braces. I'm making monthly payments on my own. Beauty has its price.

Portrait: G—

CHAPTER NINE

WHO WE ARE
G——

G—— *moved from Seoul, South Korea, to a suburb of Los Angeles, California, with her parents and older brother. For much of the time, the family was here on her father's visa. When the visa expired, they became undocumented. G—— had to grow up fast.*

When I was eight, my dad was invited to a university in Texas with a two-year contract as a visiting professor. We went along as his dependents.

Before we came here, my dad prepped my brother and me in English. He was a hard-core educator. We'd have spelling tests and things like that every day. We read books and highlighted things we didn't know. We had private tutors in English. So I started learning English when I was six. My first words were *pen, pencil,* and *monkey.*

When we landed in America, Dad said that we should live in L.A., where there are more Korean people and where we would feel more at home. He said that he would come back and forth. He helped us settle into an apartment, bought us a car, opened bank accounts, and did whatever he needed to do to make sure we would be okay. During winter and spring breaks and over the summer, he visited us. We never visited him in Texas because my brother and I were in school.

My mom didn't speak English and didn't have any friends here. My older brother, C—, and I were in school all day. Life was lonely for her. She had not learned to drive in Korea because she always took taxis everywhere. She realized that for her to survive and be less isolated, she had to learn to drive. She failed her driving test four times but passed on her fifth try. We laugh about that now. But when we run errands together, I say, "Mom, I'm the driver." I can't say I trust her driving. Ha!

We weren't among the super-well-off families in Korea, but we lived in a pretty good neighborhood. Most people there live in high-rise apartments because of the dense population. Ours was a four-bedroom apartment on the fifteenth floor. I think my mom was shocked to see such small apartments in America. We found a two-bedroom, two-bath apartment. We all thought it would be a temporary thing. Fifteen years later, we're still there.

Mom started going to an English-language school every morning, from eight to eleven. I think it was her way of wanting to better herself. Or maybe it was her desire to feel less alone. Then she'd pick us up from the elementary school, even though it was only three blocks away. We ate dinner and then went to the library to do our homework and read. My mom just loves the library.

In my elementary school, I think we had ten, fifteen Koreans. All the teachers were Caucasian. Students were mostly Armenian and some Latinos. I knew I was different because I looked different. In Korea, where 99 percent of the population is Korean, no one looks different.

There was one Korean boy in my class. At first, we didn't speak English. We didn't know the rules for kickball. We didn't know the rules for Prisoner. We didn't know the rules for anything. We were, like, what do we do? The kids would pull their eyes back and say things like "Ching Chong China."

"I'M KOREAN!" I'd shout. I'm proud of my heritage. I was more upset that they thought I was from China than about the teasing.

My second year here, Dad signed me up for a softball team. He thought it would be good exercise, a place to make friends, and a chance to speak English. I played softball and basketball. The girls I met there are still my friends.

My fourth-grade teacher was phenomenal. He has two kids that I used to babysit. He said that when I first came into his classroom, I was shy and timid and didn't say much. Toward the end of the year, I became dynamic and outgoing, and he couldn't get me to shut up. I loved school here.

When my dad's contract was up and he was about to return to Korea, my parents had to make a decision about us. My mom said, "The kids want to stay here. What can we do?" Dad went back to Korea, and Mom stayed here with us. Once Dad left, we applied for a visa extension. By then I was ten. The U.S. government gave us a two-year extension to figure out what to do. There never was a real plan. It was like, we'll figure this out as we go along. That might have been the downfall.

When I reached the seventh grade, the extension was about to run out. We went to an immigration attorney. Dad wired money to pay him. One day, my mom looked at her statement and said, "Why did the attorney buy jewelry with our credit-card information?" We called and called him to find out what was happening. He never answered. He had scammed us. He took the money and disappeared. We weren't the only Korean family he did that to.

Everything Stopped

Dad used to visit us every four or five months. By the time I was in middle school, he stopped coming. He completely stopped contacting us. That's right, he just disappeared. And things got really complicated because my mom was trying to do her best with what little money she made. My mom started working when I was in the sixth grade. I thought it was because she wanted to be more socially active and have a sense of independence. She never told us how badly we needed money, because she didn't want us to worry. She wanted us to have a normal childhood.

Mom worked at a video store. It's not that she thought that the job was beneath her, but once she said, "I can't believe how I went to college to end up doing this in my life." She was there for a couple of years. She rarely complained. When tough things come at her, she grits her teeth and gets it done without a single complaint. You would never know that she worked seventy-plus hours a week. She was always smiling and laughing.

When I started eighth grade, mom worked as a cashier at a mall right near my school. When I was in ninth grade, she picked up another job in addition to her first one. So she'd go to work at nine in the morning, come home at three, make dinner for us, and leave again at four thirty and work until the store closed, around eleven thirty at night. She got home after midnight. And she did that six days a week all through my high-school years. My brother and I rarely saw her. We were on our own. And we were fighting all the time.

Here's the thing about my brother in those days. He treated me like a younger brother, not a younger sister. We wrestled all the time. I was such a tomboy anyway, and this seemed normal. Academically, I did better than he did, and I found myself constantly belittling him. I felt like our value was based on our grades, so I would say things to upset him. Obviously he didn't like that at all. My Korean friends called their older brothers *oppa*. *Oppa* means "dad" and *umma* means "mom." I never called my brother *oppa*. I was a brat, lecturing my own brother: "C—, you can't do that! C—, you've got to up your grades."

My brother went through a rebellious stage, skipping school. Our mom had no idea this was happening, because she was always at work. She thought that her little babies could never do anything wrong.

When I was in tenth grade, my brother's AP stats teacher saw me in the hall and asked, "G——, what are you doing here?"

"What do you mean?"

"Your brother said that the whole family was going to Korea for two weeks and he would be out of school." I'm thinking, are you kidding me, C——?

My brother pulled stunts like that right and left. He once got caught reading in a Barnes & Noble near our high school. It's not like he went somewhere crazy, like drinking or anything. He was at Barnes & Noble reading because he didn't want to be at school. I think C—— got a little lost along the way. Maybe it was the loss of a father figure. He didn't have a father figure, and our mom was always working. Maybe he was cutting school for attention. I don't know.

I'm twenty-four, and I feel that I'm old enough to talk about what happened to us as a family. The thing about Korean families is that everything's so hush-hush. Anything that's not acceptable in society is ignored. It's so patriarchal — my dad was never wrong even if he was wrong. Not contacting us, not helping us, was wrong. I literally spent all my high-school years hating him.

Identity Crisis

Once I became a teenager, the relationship with my mom grew rough. I felt that she favored my brother. That was silly of me. I wanted to talk to my mom, but she was always working. I felt that my parents didn't really want us. I often fought with my brother and did very little to help out the family. And yet, in school I was a bubbly person with a diverse circle of friends. By ninth grade I joined the all-honors classes. I was a scholar athlete, associate student body president, and prom queen. My friends in high school didn't know my dad existed, because I never talked about him.

Although I was successful in school and had lots of friends, I was having my own private identity crisis. I was rebelling against my culture. I didn't know how much of my Korean culture to embrace and how much American culture to take in. At first, I accepted my Korean culture 100 percent. I only ate Korean food, spoke Korean at home, and celebrated Korean holidays. That changed because I had no Korean friends in elementary and middle school. I stopped speaking Korean at home because my mom was never there and my brother and I only spoke English to each other. My identity shifted. When I saw how irresponsible my dad was and how powerful my mom was, I began to question the woman's role in Korean culture. I became what I am to this day, a Korean-American. But then my American lifestyle collided with Mom's Korean standards.

My mom wanted me to be well dressed. I was a tomboy who wanted to go to school in basketball shorts. "Why can't I dress the way I want to dress?"

"No, no, no, when people see you, they'll think you're dressing like that because you don't have a dad and we're poor. You can't do that."

I felt that she only cared about what others thought about us, about our image. But in fact, she didn't want us to miss out on wearing what she thought other kids wore. And she didn't want us to miss out on what other kids did. For example, my brother played football and I joined the choir. Both activities were expensive. She never said no to our extracurricular activities. She did everything to give us a happy life. We took her for granted.

I hated my mom working a block and a half from my school. Every high-school student she'd see, she'd say, "I'm G—'s mom." I was so ashamed.

"Oh, my God! Stop telling everybody you're my mom!"

I actually cried about that. "Oh, Mom, I don't want to be known as . . . as . . ." I'm sorry. I'm sorry to be crying. I mean . . . look at me . . . this is so bad. I was so mean to her. I'm all right. I'm all right. I just need to get through this.

Once a kid said to my mom, "Oh, I saw G— with her boyfriend holding hands outside school."

My mom called me and said, "You are not to hold hands, kiss him, or anything in public!"

148

"I CAN DO WHATEVER I WANT!"

It felt as if she was micromanaging my relationship. I knew that culturally that's what Korean moms do. It was hard to grasp her morality when I had friends who were having sex left and right. And I thought, at least I'm not having sex. But I wasn't going to tell my mom that, right? I wish she had given me a reason why I couldn't kiss my boyfriend in public — not that I would have understood whatever she said. It's normal for kids to date. It's normal to go out to movies Friday nights. It was normal for me to grab dinner with his family. But my mom needed a reason, a what and a who and a when. Everything had to be detailed. That's normal in Korea but not here in L.A.

"Why are you texting me every two seconds to find out who I'm with and what I'm doing? DON'T YOU TRUST ME?" I'd scream, typing in upper case. I thought she was always checking up on me.

Then there was this thing with grades. When I got my SATs, even though they were higher than my diagnostic tests, she expected more. She took my phone away. I was forbidden to see my boyfriend.

"THAT'S NOT NORMAL!" I told her. "That's not normal, Mom. You don't do that to people." But she wouldn't budge.

I thought part of her acting this way was for her own image. "I have a daughter who did this! I have a daughter who won that!" I didn't feel that it was about me. It was about her. I knew she cared about me, but at sixteen, I felt that she didn't care about me as much as she cared about how others saw me.

Dad

In the middle of my senior year in high school, I started sending my dad e-mails once a week. They were lengthy e-mails. I was very angry. I said things like "I don't know what you're doing. I honestly don't effing care what you're doing, but you need to wake up. This is not fair. It was your choice to come here. It was your choice to go back. Mom's stuck, working ridiculous hours."

My dad actually responded to an e-mail. I was shocked. He said, "I'm sorry. I wish I could explain what's happening right now, but I can't.

I hope one day I can say this in person." I was so relieved. At that point I had been thinking, what has my dad been doing all this time? Is he even alive? The fact that he responded, I thought, okay, that's good. I wished he had said a little more, but at least he responded.

Undocumented

> When there were no more visa extensions, G—'s mother went to work for a church so that she would be eligible for a new visa. The family drove to the U.S. Embassy in Mexico, where her mom used her Korean passport to apply for her own visa. They reentered the country in Arizona. In time, the new visa expired too, and G—, C—, and their mother became undocumented.

When the second visa expired, I asked my mom, "What does that mean?" She said that we were lucky that we live in California and could go to college paying in-state tuition. "But from here on out, there will be a lot of restrictions. For example, you can't go to school out of state." I wanted to go to Syracuse University in New York. People from out of state paid much higher prices. Much higher!

My brother researched what we could and could not do. He came to the conclusion that to the United States government we no longer belonged here. That was totally weird to me. Why can't we be just normal? "Our family is so broken, C—. Why is this one more layer of complication? Can't this be just a little simpler?"

We couldn't both afford UC, so C— opted to go to a community college and then transfer. Even though California allowed for in-state tuition for all students, college was still too expensive. If you include books, board, and tuition, it comes to about twelve thousand dollars a year. My mom was making eight dollars an hour, working sixty-plus hours a week. Even with part-time jobs we couldn't afford tuition.

I applied to college, and what do you know? I got accepted.

"Why can't we just be normal?"

Since my brother had been accepted to the same school and we couldn't send him, I decided to go to a community college and then transfer. But my brother said that if we both end up going to community college, people who don't know our story would assume that we didn't try hard enough. "Mom sacrificed nine years for us to be here. For her sake, at the very least, one of us should go to college at the right time."

That's an example of where the image part of my culture comes in. I don't want to generalize and say this about all Koreans, or all Korean-Americans, but at least the ones in my mother's circle are really big on names. This kind of conversation happens all the time:

"Oh, your daughter got into UC-what?"

"UCLA."

"On scholarship?"

"Yes."

"Oh, wow. What was her GPA?"

It was all a numbers game.

My mom's family owned land in Korea. When my maternal grandparents passed away, they gave each child a piece of the land. My mom was waiting for the land prices to pick up. But she had to pay for tuition. She sold the land, her engagement ring, and things like that. And she continued working to put both of us through college.

Later in my freshman year, my mom said, "Enjoy college! Don't worry about a thing." I really milked it. I don't think I ever realized how difficult it was to make a living. It was so easy for me to ask my mom for money. "Hey, Mom, the basketball camp is going to cost three hundred bucks." "Hey, Mom, the choir trip to New York is fourteen hundred dollars." And she paid it. I saw my mom working night and day, but there was a disconnect between her work and my wants.

Once my brother finished community college, we both went to the same college at the same time. That meant twice the tuition at once. So my brother said, "I'm going to work for a year and you go." He insisted that I go off to college. That was beyond me. It was a huge sacrifice.

Graduation was just around the corner. Guess who decided to show up?

Gone for So Long

I was a nervous wreck going to the airport with my brother to pick up my father. I was shaking. There was so much bitterness and anger, but at the same time, I was excited to see him. It had been five years since I had last seen him. I felt, though, that if I showed that I was excited to see him, he would think it was okay to have been gone for so long. So I tried hard not to be emotional.

He stayed at our house for three days, sleeping in the living room. Everyone pretended that everything was great. In my family we do an exceptional job pretending that everything is okay.

During my first year of college, my dad visited during the school's family weekend. Sophomore year, I kept in touch with him via e-mail. He called our house. But he didn't support us financially at all.

From my sophomore year of college to the middle of my junior year, he cut off all contact again. For the rest of my junior year he was present. When I was about to graduate, he didn't talk to us again. Now we're on the downside. My dad hasn't talked to us in a year and three months.

My parents are still legally married. That's another thing about Korean culture. Divorce is looked down upon. "I don't understand," I said to my mom. "You could be so happy. If you remarried, you wouldn't have to work ridiculous hours. You should have cut it off nine years ago."

College Transformation

College went by fast. I loved it. In college I finally realized I couldn't be a bratty sixteen-year-old, asking for things and complaining all the time. It took going away to college to change my feelings toward my mother. I realized all that she had done for me.

I graduated early because it would lessen the load on my mom. I took twenty-two units my sophomore and junior year and graduated a little early. (Students are considered full-time at twelve units.) I majored in international studies and sociology. I learned that I was capable of doing a lot of different things. I was working.

The summer after my sophomore year, my brother and I were both back in L.A., trying to work a lot of different jobs. My brother found a night job cleaning places. He'd leave our house at ten thirty p.m. and come home about seven a.m. He reeked of chemicals. But it paid good money, twenty-something an hour. He was paid at the end of the week. By week three, he wasn't paid. They said that they'd pay him the next week. But he never got paid, because the person who hired him ran off with the money. He couldn't go to the law because he was undocumented.

He didn't know what to do. He was so angry. I've never seen him so angry. He refused to leave the house. That's when he made up his mind that he wasn't going to stay in America, because it sucked.

As that was happening to C——, a Korean lady who owned a group of all-night restaurants was looking for workers. At first she gave me the run-around. Then she gave me a job in another community, in Santa Monica. I couldn't drive, but I told her I had a brother who could drive. "Could you give him a job too?"

Long story short, we worked there for a week. We'd go in at one a.m., and leave at five thirty a.m. After a week, she called us and said that it wasn't going to work out with us.

"Why not?"

"Well, the restaurant is not that busy at that hour. And people are complaining that with two more people working, there's less tip money."

"Okay, I get it." I was respectful. She had offered me a job, so I had to be nice. I said, "Well, what about the pay for this week?"

She said, "We'll figure it out." A red flag went up.

"No. We're going to figure it out right now." I couldn't believe I was speaking to a Korean woman so forcefully.

"I'm busy now."

"It's five o'clock in the morning. What are you doing?"

"I'm in a different branch. Come back tomorrow night at one." We drove late at night to get to Santa Monica. The lady didn't show up until three a.m. I was really pissed, and I told her off. She said, "You can't be that angry at me. I took a chance on you guys. You are here illegally."

I was so ashamed, because she was Korean. I was so frustrated, I could hardly talk. "You tell us to come when you want us to come. You tell us to go when you want us to go. Nobody is happy working here for you. You treat everybody like crap. You can't do this. And if you want me to apologize, I won't." By the way, I was dropping F-bombs every which way. I was just so livid. My brother was yelling, "Stop."

"I am not stopping," I shouted back to him. I was too outraged. After a while, she gave us the money she owed us. She said, "I hope I never see you again."

"I hope I never see you."

Choices

It became clear that my brother was moving back to Korea. He said, "There's no reason to stay. There are too many things I can't do here."

I couldn't see packing up and leaving the place I've lived in for more than half my life. I came here when I was eight. I was twenty-one and graduating college. I've lived here for thirteen years. I didn't want to leave.

"Okay, that's your choice," I told him.

But then it was so ironic that the day before our graduation, President Obama made that announcement about DACA. "It's a sign from God, C——. You are staying. You are staying."

He said, "No, there are still too many restrictions. You need to re-apply every two years. You can't travel out of the country without advanced parole."

"But those are the things we didn't have anyway!" I was focusing on the positive and really, really happy about what we could do.

"G——, they're still treating us like criminals. Really? You need to apply before going anywhere? That's not normal."

"I guess. But I'm still stuck on what I *can* do. I can drive! I can work!"

Long story short, we both applied for DACA at the urging of my mom. But my brother left before he even heard anything.

American culture has changed me. I've lived here for fifteen years, and I lived in Korea for eight. Mathematically I'm more in tune with American culture than Korean culture. But I'm very proud of who I am, my roots, my inner-core values. I feel most comfortable identifying myself

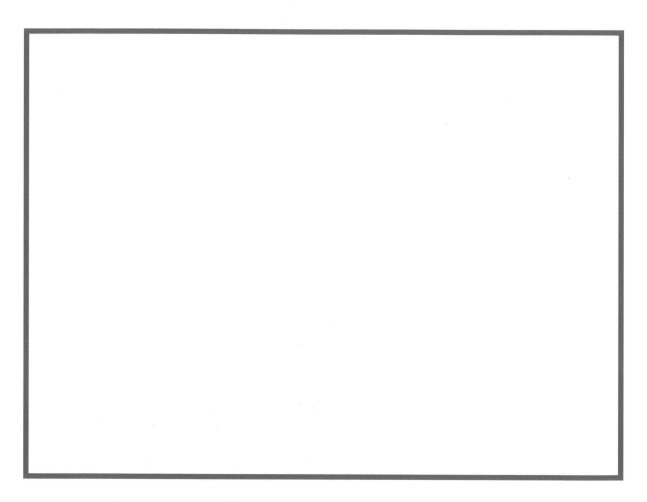

"the freedom to identify ourselves as who we are"

as a Korean-American. I don't think it will ever be a perfect balance. All I know is, we have the freedom to identify ourselves as who we are, as who we want to be.

My mom and I have become very close. We talk on the phone every night. I look forward to our conversations. There are times, though, when she still calls me out on things. I told her I wanted to get a master's in education.

"Why not law school?'

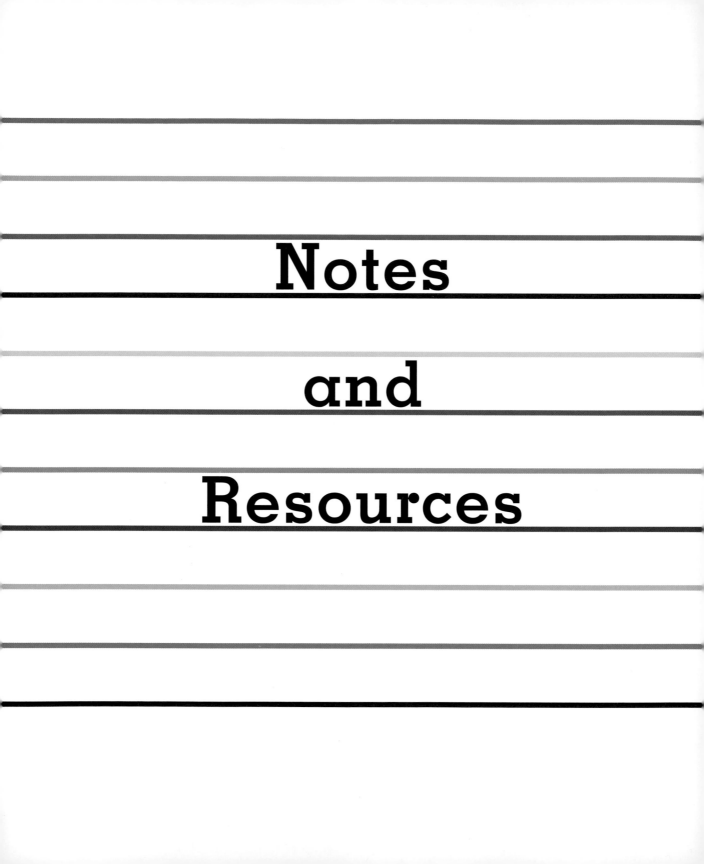

Notes

and

Resources

UNITED STATES IMMIGRATION LAW
AND EXECUTIVE ACTIONS

From 1790 to 2017

The following material comes in part, with editing, from the Migration Policy Institute and ProCon.org. www.migrationpolicy.org/research/timeline-1790 and http://immigration.procon.org/view.timeline.php?timelineID=000023

1790: The Naturalization Act established the country's first uniform law for "free white persons" who had resided in the United States for at least two years by granting them citizenship as long as they demonstrated good moral character and swore allegiance to the Constitution.

1798: The Alien and Sedition Acts encompassed four laws that contained a number of strict immigration enforcement provisions: An Act to Establish an Uniform Rule of Naturalization, An Act Concerning Aliens, An Act Respecting Alien Enemies, and An Act for the Punishment of Certain Crimes against the United States. These acts increased the residency requirement for American citizenship from five to fourteen years, authorized the president to imprison or deport aliens considered "dangerous to the peace and safety of the United States," and restricted speech critical of the government.

1882: The Chinese Exclusion Act was the United States' first attempt to regulate immigration along racial lines.

1888: The Scott Act further restricted Chinese nationals who departed the United States from returning.

1917: The Immigration Act created an "Asiatic barred zone," which included British India, most of Southeast Asia, and almost all of the Middle East. The law exempted students, teachers, government officers, lawyers, physicians, and chemists and their dependents.

1921: The Emergency Quota Act limited the number of immigrants from any country to 3 percent of those already in the United States as of the 1910 census.

1924: The National Origins Quota Act, commonly known as the **Johnson-Reed Act,** limited European immigration to 150,000 per year, and reduced each nationality's allowance to 2 percent of its U.S. population in the 1890 census. Because significantly fewer southern and eastern Europeans were recorded in the 1890 census, this act effectively reduced immigration from these regions while making more room than was necessary for countries like Great Britain.

1942: The Bracero Agreement was prompted by labor shortages of World War II. The United States allowed Mexican nationals to enter the country as temporary agricultural workers. This agreement was extended in 1949 and 1951. The program continued in some form until 1964.

1942: The Magnuson Act repealed the Chinese Exclusion Act and allowed Chinese nationals to become U.S. citizens.

1945: The War Brides Act authorized the admission of foreign-born spouses and children of U.S. citizens who served in or were honorably discharged from the military during World War II.

1948: The Displaced Persons Act allowed more than 200,000 persons displaced from their homeland by Nazi persecution to immigrate to the United States.

1952: The Immigration and Nationality Act (INA), more commonly known as the **McCarran-Walter Act,** created the modern immigration act by consolidating several immigration laws into one statute. It removed all racial barriers to immigration but retained the national origins quotas.

1953: The Refugee Relief Act authorized the admission of up to 205,000 non-quota immigrants who were fleeing persecution in Europe.

1962: The Migration and Refugee Assistance Act authorized funds to help foreign nationals from the Western Hemisphere who had fled their countries of origin due to persecution or a fear of persecution based on race, religion, or political opinion. This law, signed by President John F. Kennedy, was intended to assist Cuban nationals fleeing the Castro regime.

1965: The Immigration and Nationality Act, known as the **Hart-Celler Act,** abolished the national-origins quota system and replaced it with a system that admitted immigrants based on their relationship to a U.S. citizen, lawful permanent resident, or U.S. employer.

1975: The Indochina Migration and Refugee Assistance Act expanded the definition of the term *refugee* to include individuals who were fleeing persecution or fear of persecution from Cambodia and Vietnam.

1980: The Refugee Act allowed individuals to seek asylum in the United States if they were fleeing persecution or a well-founded fear of persecution on account of race, religion, nationality, membership in a particular social group, or political opinion. This act brought U.S. law into compliance with international law.

1986: The Immigration Reform and Control Act increased the Border Patrol and imposed sanctions on employers who knowingly hired or recruited unauthorized immigrants. It also allowed unauthorized immigrants who had lived in the United States since 1982 to regularize their status.

1996: The Antiterrorism and Effective Death Penalty Act added new crimes to the definition of *aggravated felony.* (In U.S. immigration law, an aggravated felony, or *violent felony,* refers to a broad category of criminal offenses that carry certain severe consequences for those seeking asylum, legal permanent resident status, citizenship, or avoidance of deportation proceedings.) It established the "expedited removal" procedure for arriving noncitizens that border officials suspected lacked the proper entry documents or were engaged in fraud. This procedure was amended the same year by the Illegal Immigration Reform and Immigrant Responsibility Act.

1996: The Illegal Immigration Reform and Immigrant Responsibility Act added new grounds for nonadmission and deportation and expanded the list of crimes that would constitute an aggravated felony. It also created expedited removal procedures and reduced the scope of the judicial review of immigration decisions. The law expanded the mandatory detention of immigrants in standard removal proceedings if they had previously been convicted of certain criminal offenses. It also increased the number of Border Patrol agents, introduced new border control measures, reduced government benefits that were available for immigrants (as did the welfare reform measures enacted the same year), increased the penalties for unauthorized immigrants, toughened the procedural requirements for asylum seekers and other immigrants, mandated an entry-exit system designed to monitor both the arrivals and departures of immigrants, and established a new program by which employers and social service agencies could verify the eligibility of immigrants.

1997: The Nicaraguan Adjustment and Central American Relief Act provided several avenues for relief from deportation and adjustment of status for qualified immigrants from Nicaragua, Cuba, El Salvador, Guatemala, and the former Soviet-bloc countries. The following year, benefits were expanded to include Haiti.

2001: The USA Patriot Act expanded the terrorism grounds for excluding immigrants from entering the United States and increased the monitoring of foreign students.

2002: The Homeland Security Act created the Department of Homeland Security. The following year, all immigration services were restructured into three new agencies: Customs and Border Protection (CBP), Immigration and Customs Enforcement (ICE), and the U.S. Citizenship and Immigration Services (USCIS).

2005: The REAL ID Act established terrorism-related grounds for inadmissibility and deportation, included measures to improve border infrastructure, and required states to verify an applicant's legal status before issuing a driver's license or personal I.D. card.

2006: The Secure Fence Act mandated the construction of more than seven hundred miles of double-reinforced fence to be built along the border with Mexico.

2012: Deferred Action for Childhood Arrivals (DACA) is an executive action announced by President Barack Obama that states that certain people who came to the United States as children and meet several guidelines may request deferred action for a period of two years, subject to renewal. Congress has not voted the Deferred Action for Childhood Arrivals into law.

2017: The Trump Administration formally announced the end of DACA.

CHAPTER NOTES

These notes include background information, law, commentary, resources, and websites that relate to each chapter. The laws discussed in the notes were in place during the time of the participants' interviews. They may have changed since then.

Title

The book's title, *We Are Here to Stay,* is inspired by #heretostay. It is a message from undocumented immigrants that "This is our home, we are part of our communities, and we aren't going to be forced out." It is a message of power, community, resilience, and resistance.

To the Reader

p. viii: DACA was a two-year program, subject to renewal, that allowed temporary relief from deportation to undocumented persons between the ages of fifteen and thirty-one who have lived in the United States continuously for at least five years. It enabled them to have a Social Security number so that they could work legally. The guidelines were strict: applicants had to have attended school or graduated, obtained a general education development (GED) certificate, or been honorably discharged from the coast guard or armed forces; they could not have been convicted of a felony, significant misdemeanor, or three or more misdemeanors; and they could not have posed a threat to national security or public safety. This program was not a path to citizenship. It was an executive action, not a law in the traditional sense. The courts, Congress, or the president could undo DACA.

p. viii: Additional information about Deferred Action for Childhood Arrivals (DACA) can be found at the U.S. Citizenship and Immigration Services website: https://www.uscis.gov/humanitarian/consideration-deferred-action-childhood-arrivals-daca.

p. ix: "It is an executive action, not a law": Some executive actions, such as agreements, policies, guidelines, or other decisions made by governors or by the president, have the force of law. Other forms of executive action include granting pardons, designating disaster areas eligible for emergency relief, designating national monuments, and setting priorities for enforcing the law.

PART ONE: COMING TO AMERICA
Chapter One: *La Familia,* Part I

p. 6: "We wanted to immigrate to the U.S. . . . . But the law had changed": At the time this book was written, family-based immigration and employment-based immigration are the two main avenues for individuals to become lawful permanent residents (LPRs, or green card holders) in the United States. Employment-based immigration is generally limited to highly skilled employees. Family-based immigration requires a family member in the United States who is a U.S. citizen or lawful permanent resident to petition on behalf of a close family relative outside the United States. There are numerical limits on family-based immigration, and the family member must fall within certain specified relationships. For more information on the categories, the numbers of people allotted to each category, and the waiting times, visit https://travel.state.gov/content/travel/en/legal/visa-law0 /visa-bulletin/2016/visa-bulletin-for-january-2016.html.

p. 10: *La Estrella* translates to "The Star."

p. 13: The Universal Declaration of Human Rights was adopted by the United Nations General Assembly on December 10, 1948. It was the first global expression of what people believed were the inherent rights of human beings. www.un.org/en /universal-declaration-human-rights/.

p. 16: "'You should get married'": In general, a person may qualify for naturalization if the person has been a lawful permanent resident (LPR, a green card holder) of the United States for five years and has met other eligibility requirements, such as understanding English, knowing the history and principles of the U.S. government, and having good moral character. Lawful permanent residents who are married to a U.S. citizen can apply for naturalization after three years if they have been living in marital union with the same U.S. spouse during this time and meet all the other eligibility requirements. www.uscis.gov /us-citizenship/citizenship-through-naturalization/naturalization-spouses-us-citizens.

p. 18: The DREAM Act immigration legislation: To learn more about the DREAM Act, visit www.americanimmigrationcouncil.org/research/guide-s744-understanding-2013 -senate-immigration-bill.

Chapter Two: *La Familia,* Part II

p. 27: "During my junior year in high school, I connected with . . . program": The program referred to is a national, not-for-profit organization dedicated to identifying exceptional public high-school students from socioeconomically disadvantaged backgrounds. This organization no longer includes undocumented immigrants. Former participants are currently working to change this policy. The website for this organization is intentionally hidden.

p. 30: DREAMer: DREAMers stands for Development, Relief, and Education for Alien Minors. More information about the DREAMers can be found at the United We Dream website, http://unitedwedream.org.

p. 30: "In 2010, our group of DREAMers … in front of Congress": The DREAM Act was legislation that would have provided a road to provisional resident status to those who could meet the following conditions: had proof that they entered the United States before age sixteen and had lived here at least five years; they had graduated from a U.S. high school or had received a GED; they had passed criminal background checks and reviews; and they had demonstrated good moral character. Various legislative proposals known as the Development, Relief, and Education for Alien Minors (DREAM) Act have been introduced in the U.S. Senate and House of Representatives since 2001. The House passed a DREAM Act bill in 2010 by a vote of 216–198 but failed to reach the sixty votes needed to prevent a filibuster in the Senate.

p. 36: "She didn't have . . . parole to leave": DACA holders can leave the country, but they must apply for advance parole, which is basically permission to travel abroad and return to the United States. Early on, DACA holders could apply for permission to leave the country and then return, but most people did not. It is assumed that they either didn't know about this part of DACA or were fearful about applying.

Chapter Three: No More Deaths: A Photo-Essay

This photo-essay was shot digitally during the daytime. Using Photoshop software, the images were converted to black-and-white or computer-generated infrared. Infrared conversion creates a completely different effect in photography. Green appears white, and blue appears black. This technique was used in the landscape photographs to replicate what the migrants experienced during their nighttime walks.

p. 42: "They stayed in the United States and saved their money to hire *coyotes*": A *coyote* is an unofficial or underground guide who is paid to lead immigrants through the desert.

Chapter Four: We Saw a Rabbit

P— and I met through her lawyers at Atlas: DIY. DIY stands for "Do It Yourself." Atlas: DIY's mission statement describes its organization as "unlocking immigrant youth's access to legal services, leadership development, and learning opportunities in a space owned, run, and governed by the youth themselves." When the organization moved to new offices, P— was one of the volunteers who helped with the construction. www.atlasdiy.org/local/about/what-is-atlasdiy/.

p. 62: "Before, I only wore *huaraches*": *Huaraches* are a type of handmade sandals.

p. 63: "I was scared because we'd heard . . . about the *pandillas*": *Pandillas* is Spanish for "gangs."

p. 65: "One time when we were making *frijoles*": *Frijoles* is a Mexican dish usually made with kidney beans or black beans.

p. 74: "It's called the Door . . . Rebecca McBride": The Door is an organization that helps youths in New York City gain the tools they need to become successful in school, in work, and in life. www.door.org.

p. 74: "I realized then . . . Special Immigrant Juvenile Status (SIJS)": Special Immigrant Juvenile Status is a form of immigration relief that eventually leads to lawful permanent residency in the United States. Its purpose is to help foreign children living in the United States who have been abused, abandoned, or neglected. www.uscis.gov/green-card/sij.

p. 74: "Those who receive SIJSs . . . path toward lawful permanent residency": A lawful permanent resident (LPR), also referred to as a green card holder, is someone who has been granted authorization to live and work in the United States on a permanent basis and can eventually apply to become a U.S. citizen. A person can become a permanent resident in one of several ways. Most individuals are sponsored by a family member or employer in the United States. Other individuals may become permanent residents through refugee or asylum status or other humanitarian programs. For additional information, go to www.uscis.gov/greencard.

Chapter Five: Under My Shadow

p. 80: "My *tía* from Arizona agreed to meet . . . at the border": *Tía* is Spanish for "aunt."

p. 88: "During my senior year, people from the Arizona DREAM Act Coalition . . . undocumented immigrants": The Arizona DREAM Act Coalition is an immigrant youth-led organization that focuses on the fight for higher education and for immigrant rights. http://theadac.org.

p. 88: "But then the governor of Arizona . . . driver's license at that time": The ACLU went to court and blocked the driver's license ban in Arizona. DACA recipients have had the right to a driver's license in Arizona as of December 2014. http://kjzz.org/content/92644 /judge-dreamers-can-keep-arizona-drivers-licenses; and www.aclu.org/news/federal -court-permanently-blocks-arizona-ban-dreamers-licenses/. In May 2015, the Arizona Board of Regents adopted a policy allowing DACA recipients who meet other residency requirements to pay in-state tuition rates at public colleges under its jurisdiction. Arizona's attorney general has appealed this decision. www.azcentral.com/story/news /politics/immigration/2015/05/07/regents-dreamers-pay-state-tuition/70951416/.

p. 88: "She told me about QUIP": QUIP is a program that works to "organize and empower undocumented lesbian, gay, bisexual, transgender, and queer immigrants, and allies. Its members address social and systemic barriers that affect themselves and the broader LGBTQ and immigrant community." http://unitedwedream.org/?s=quip.

PART TWO: TWISTS AND TURNS
Chapter Six: Lucky Breaks
J— and I met through his lawyer, Lauren Burke, the director of Atlas: DIY. www.atlasdiy.org/local/about/what-is-atlasdiy.

p. 94: "Does Mr. X live here?" To protect J—'s family's privacy, his father is referred to as Mr. X.

p. 98: "I had never worked": Labor laws in Ghana do not allow a child under fifteen to take a full-time job. In the United States, according to the Fair Labor Standards Act of 1938, sixteen is the basic minimum age for employment in any occupation other than ones declared by the secretary of labor to be hazardous. Fourteen is the minimum age for employment in specific occupations outside of school hours for limited periods of time each day and week. Eighteen is the minimum age for employment in nonagricultural occupations declared hazardous by the secretary of labor. There are no standard age restrictions for youths who deliver newspapers; perform in radio, television, movie, or theatrical productions; work in businesses owned by their parents (except in mining, manufacturing, or hazardous jobs); and perform babysitting or minor chores around a private home. (Some state laws have extended restrictions to sixteen- and seventeen-year-olds.) www.dol.gov/general/topic/youthlabor.

p. 99: "I tried to pray five times a day, the way I did in Ghana": Muslims pray five times a day to ensure a personal connection with and remembrance of God throughout the day. *Salat,* or prayer, is one of the Five Pillars of Islam, and an obligatory religious duty for every Muslim. It is a physical, mental, and spiritual act of worship that is observed five times every day at prescribed times. www.islam-guide.com/ch3-16.htm.

p. 107: "Well, let's speak Twi": There are three major languages in Ghana: Twi, Ga, and English. J—'s family speaks Ga. Although he knows all three languages, J— speaks mostly English.

p. 112: "Because I was undocumented . . . I couldn't travel out of the country": J— was not eligible for DACA because he had not lived continuously in the United States since June 15, 2007.

p. 115: "Lauren filed a T visa, for victims of trafficking": The T nonimmigrant status (the T visa) that J— talks about is for noncitizens who have been the victims of severe forms of human trafficking. Children under the age of twenty-one who apply for the T visa can apply for their parents and unmarried siblings under eighteen to receive derivative status, which is what J— is referring to when he says that he can apply for his family to come and visit. www.uscis.gov/humanitarian/victims-human -trafficking-other-crimes/victims-human-trafficking-t-nonimmigrant-status/questions -and-answers-victims-human-trafficking-t-nonimmigrant-status-0.

Chapter Seven: The American Dream Is So Powerful

p. 119: A *tithe* is 10 percent of a family's earnings that goes to the church.

p. 119: "The Calling": A calling is an inner urge or strong impulse, especially referring to one believed to be divinely inspired.

p. 119: The Congregational Christian Church of Samoa: The CCCS traces its beginnings to the 1830 arrival of missionaries sent by the London Missionary Society, accompanied by missionary teachers from Tahiti and the Cook Islands and a Samoan couple from Tonga. Within a few years, virtually the whole of Samoa was converted to Christianity. www.cccs.org.ws.

p. 122: "When the visas ran out, we stayed in L.A.": *Visa overstay* means staying in the country beyond the expected date on one's U.S. visa. www.alllaw.com/articles/nolo /us-immigration/consequences-of-overstaying-on-temporary-visa.html.

Chapter Eight: Go Big or Go Home

p. 130: "We pay our taxes": According to the American Immigration Council, undocumented immigrants pay taxes, in the form of income, property, sales, and taxes at the federal and state level. The Social Security Administration has a "suspense file" (taxes that cannot be matched to workers' names and Social Security numbers), which grew by $20 billion between 1990 and 1998. www.americanimmigrationcouncil.org/research /unauthorized-immigrants-pay-taxes-too.

p. 133: "He taught me how to follow the Scout oath": The Boy Scout oath: "On my honor I will do my best to do my duty to God and my country and to obey the Scout Law; to help other people at all times; to keep myself physically strong, mentally awake, and morally straight."

p. 137: "The same day that President Obama gave us DACA, then-governor of Arizona Jan Brewer signed an executive order. It prohibited anyone who received Deferred Action through the president's action from getting state benefits, including driver's licenses": An executive order is one type of executive action (see note to p. ix) and is legally binding unless it violates other laws of the United States. Executive orders by the president are published in the Federal Register. Executive orders issued by state governors are published by the states. To learn more about executive orders, visit www.americanbar.org /publications/insights_on_law_andsociety/17/fall-2016/what-is-an-executive-order.html.

The American Civil Liberties Union, along with a coalition of civil rights organizations, filed a class-action lawsuit challenging Arizona Governor Jan Brewer's unconstitutional executive order, which denies driver's licenses to a specific class of immigrant youth despite their being authorized to live and work in the United States. April 5, 2016: The Ninth Circuit Court of Appeals affirmed a lower court's ruling that permanently blocks Arizona from denying driver's licenses to immigrants who have been granted Deferred Action for Childhood Arrivals. www.aclu.org/cases/ arizona-dream-act-coalition-et-al-v-brewer.

p. 137: "We won the battle getting some type of legal status": DACA gives undocumented students legal presence — or permission to live in the country — but it does not give them legal status. There's a difference between the two: *Legal status* means that the person is a U.S. resident or visa holder. *Legal presence* means that one's presence is temporarily legal as long as the individual complies with the terms of the temporary permission and with other laws of the United States. A student who doesn't renew the card is eligible for deportation. In addition, when the Deferred Action program is dismantled by another president, legislative action, or the courts, the student can be deported.

p. 140: "It was about the Joining Forces initiative": In 2011, First Lady Michelle Obama and Dr. Jill Biden launched Joining Forces, a nationwide initiative calling on all Americans to rally around service members, veterans, and their families by supporting them through providing wellness, education, and employment opportunities. Joining Forces works hand in hand with the public and private sectors to ensure that service members, veterans, and their families have the tools they need to succeed throughout their lives. https://whitehouse .gov/joiningforces/about.

Chapter Nine: Who We Are

p. 150: "When there were no more visa extensions, G— 's mother went to work for a church": Temporary-worker visas are for persons who want to enter the United States for employment for a fixed period of time, and are not considered permanent or indefinite. In order to hire someone lawfully on a visa to work temporarily, the prospective employer must generally file a nonimmigrant visa petition on the person's behalf with the U.S. Citizenship and Immigration Services (USCIS). After the visa petition is approved, the applicant can seek a visa at any U.S. embassy or consulate. www.uscis.gov /working-united-states/temporary-nonimmigrant-workers/.

p. 150: "She said that we were lucky . . . in-state tuition": On October 12, 2001, Governor Gray Davis of California signed into law a provision that allowed undocumented students who resided in California and had gone to high school there for the last three years to pay the same rate of tuition as resident Californians. http://ab540.com/What_Is_AB540_.html.

AUTHOR'S NOTE

In the late nineteenth century, four young people, separately and alone, left Russia and emigrated to America. They came for reasons similar to those of the families in this book: to escape violence and to pursue an education for themselves and their future children. They believed that the American dream would allow them the opportunity to achieve a satisfying life. Did they have money? No. Did they speak English? No. Did they have documents to make them naturalized citizens in America? I don't know. I am thankful that those four young people, my grandparents, were brave enough to leave their families and their culture for an unknown future.

The roots of one's family tree are tough to untangle. Integrated into the immigrant (success) story is what is left behind: family, history, place, language, and identity. All of us in the United States, with the exception of Native Americans, are descended from people from former countries. Either we or our ancestors know what it's like to make one's way in a foreign culture. We've had to juggle becoming "American" with respect for our heritage. And so, with Mom, Pop, Grandma, and Grandpa always in mind, I set out to learn about contemporary undocumented immigrants.

The media and politicians often talk about immigrants who are faced with deportation for one reason or another. Who are these people? Why did they come? How did they get here? I searched for individual young people whose authentic voice would lead to greater understanding of why they or their parents were disposed to come to or remain in a country whose current laws say that they are unwelcome.

Because immigration is such an enormous subject, I decided to focus on undocumented young people who have lived in this country for most of their lives. By including descriptions of their birth cultures and how they combined their backgrounds with an American lifestyle, I hoped to underline unique qualities that make our country distinct.

Once a person agreed to participate in *We Are Here to Stay,* we did a series of recorded interviews and photography sessions. I transcribed the recordings and rewrote them as narratives. To be certain that the storytelling's truth matched the participants' truth, all the interviewees were given their chapter to read and approve, a process that continued throughout numerous drafts and editing.

On November 8, 2016, Donald J. Trump became president-elect of the United States. Much of his campaign contained anti-immigration speech-making, especially about Muslims and undocumented people. America, the place my grandparents fled to for safety and security, the land that welcomed immigrants, was no longer openhearted to approximately 700,000 DACAmented students and military personnel.

When Mr. Trump became president, he canceled DACA. This meant that the DREAMers could be deported. This is why I felt that I had to use only the first initial of the contributors' names. Photographs and other identifiers have been removed.

More than ever, I'm appreciative, proud, and in awe of everyone who participated in *We Are Here to Stay*. These individuals remind me again and again that the American dream is worth fighting for — and that the American dream is worth sharing.

ACKNOWLEDGMENTS

We Are Here to Stay belongs to S—, D—, Y—, John, Kathryn, P—, C—, J—, T—, G—, and G—. Without their reflections, honesty, intelligence, warmth, bravery, and downright decency, this book could not have been written. Thank you from the bottom of my heart.

Deepest gratitude to the following people and groups who were so generously helpful:

Professor Maryellen Fullerton at Brooklyn Law School, who is an expert on asylum and refugee law, talked to me about immigration and shared fascinating information about major immigration issues. Her advice, instruction, encouragement, and friendship are present throughout this book.

Susan Herman, president of the American Civil Liberties Union (ACLU) and a professor at Brooklyn Law School, kindly introduced me to several lawyers within the ACLU who work on immigration law, including Cecillia Wang (deputy legal director) and Michael Tan (staff attorney, Immigrants' Rights Project).

Atlas: DIY: Lauren Burke (executive director and cofounder), Rebecca McBride (staff attorney), Maria Caba (director of outreach), and Michelina Ferrara (deputy director). Thanks to Lauren for the legal information in J—'s chapter, and to Rebecca for her participation and legal information in P—'s chapter.

The Lacey and Larkin Frontera Fund: Carmen Cornejo (program manager). Carmen's help, insights, and calm in response to my harried last-minute phone calls were deeply appreciated.

The National AAPI DACA (Asian American and Pacific Islander Deferred Action for Childhood Arrivals Collaborative): Ju Hong (collaborative coordinator). This organization represents ASPIRE-LA.

No More Deaths/*No Más Muertes*: Reverend John Fife (founder) and Kathryn Ferguson (volunteer). Thank you for an eye-opening visit to Sonora.

Margaret St. John and Rohn Eloul, in Tucson, Arizona, provided background information about living near the Mexican border.

The wise and accomplished readers who took the time from their demanding lives to check facts and mind the flow and shape of *We Are Here to Stay* are Maryellen Fullerton, Michael Tan, Lauren Burke, Robie Harris, Elizabeth Levy, Deborah Heiligman, Thea Lurie, Stacy Goldate, and Bailey Kuklin. If anything has fallen through the cracks, the fault is most certainly mine.

Kathleen Anderson, photographer and teacher at the International Center of Photography in New York City, reviewed my images and helped make them sparkle.

Brianne Johnson, my agent-goddess at Writers House, is more than an extraordinary agent. She gave me feedback, support, and encouragement throughout this journey. What a pleasure it is to work with you.

The commitment of everyone at Candlewick Press to *We Are Here to Stay* never wavered. It is an honor to publish with you. A special thanks to Hilary Van Dusen, editor extraordinaire. She is my rock who enables me to take artistic risks. She also produces beautiful, gutsy books.

One more thanks to my husband, Bailey. He hiked the dusty desert trails (carrying a heavy backpack filled with water for the crossers), sent me back to the computer to make a chapter "sing," questioned the legal explanations to make them clearer, listened for hours and hours of "eureka moments" that didn't quite strike gold. How lucky I am to share this life with him.

RESOURCES

BOOKS

Andreu, Maria E. *The Secret Side of Empty*. Philadelphia: Running Press Kids, 2015.

Budhos, Marina. *Ask Me No Questions*. New York: Athenaeum Books for Young Readers, 2006.

Danticat, Edwidge. *Brother, I'm Dying*. New York: Vintage, 2008.

Ferguson, Kathryn. *The Haunting of the Mexican Border: A Woman's Journey*. Albuquerque: University of New Mexico Press, 2015.

Ferguson, Kathryn, Norma A. Price, and Ted Parks. *Crossing with the Virgin: Stories from the Migrant Trail*. Tucson: University of Arizona Press, 2010.

Na, An. *A Step from Heaven*. New York: Speak, 2003.

Nazario, Sonia. *Enrique's Journey*. New York: Random House, 2007.

Nicholls, Walter J. *The DREAMers: How the Undocumented Youth Movement Transformed the Immigrant Rights Debate*. Redwood City, CA: Stanford University Press, 2013.

Yang, Gene Luen. *American Born Chinese*. New York: Square Fish, 2008.

DOCUMENTARY FILMS AND THEATER

A View from the Bridge, Arthur Miller (play).

De Novo, Jeffrey Solomon, Houses on the Moon Theater Company, 2010 (play).

Documented, Jose Antonio Vargas, 2013 (film).

Don't Tell Anyone (No Le Digas a Nadie), Mikaela Shwer, Latino Public Broadcasting and PBS, 2015 (film).

The Dream Is Now, Davis Guggenheim, 2013 (film).

How Democracy Works Now, a series of twelve films about immigration reform. Shari Robertson and Michael Camerini, 2013.

Immigration Battle, Shari Robertson and Michael Camerini, coproduced by the filmmakers, PBS, and ITVS, 2015 (film).

Walking Merchandise — Child Trafficking and the Snakehead Trade, Ethan Downing, 2013 (film).

Which Way Home, Rebecca Cammisa, 2009 (film).

WEBSITES

The following websites are useful for undocumented youths and others who are seeking immigration information.

The ACLU Immigrants' Rights Project uses targeted impact litigation, advocacy, and public outreach to protect the rights and liberties of immigrants. www.aclu.org/issues/immigrants-rights

Atlas: DIY offers a wide variety of services, such as free legal services, language classes, college preparation programs, scholarship lists, and more. www.atlasdiy.org/wabout/what-is-atlasdiy

Educators for Fair Consideration (E4FC) empowers undocumented young people in their pursuit of college, career, and citizenship. http://e4fc.org

Kids in Need of Defense (KIND) serves as the leading organization for the protection of children who enter the U.S. immigration system alone and strives to ensure that no such child appears in immigration court without representation. They achieve fundamental fairness through high-quality legal representation and by advancing the child's best interests, safety, and well-being. http://supportkind.org

The Lacey and Larkin Frontera Fund was created by Michael Lacey and Jim Larkin, cofounders of *Phoenix New Times* and Village Voice Media. They have dedicated settlement money arising out of their illegal arrest by Sheriff Joe Arpaio (Maricopa County, Arizona) to fund migrant rights organizations throughout Arizona. www.laceyandlarkinfronterafund.org

The National Immigration Law Center (NILC) is the primary advocacy organization in the United States dedicated to defending and advancing the rights and opportunities of low-income immigrants and their families. www.nilc.org

No More Deaths/*No Más Muertes* defines its mission as follows: "To end death and suffering in the Mexico-U.S. borderlands through civil initiative: people of conscience working openly and in community to uphold fundamental human rights." http://forms.nomoredeaths.org

The Safe Passage Project addresses the unmet needs of immigrant children living in New York "by providing legal representation to empower each child to pursue a safe, stable future. We recruit, train, and mentor volunteer attorneys for unaccompanied minors in immigration court. Without us, many of these children would be unrepresented and unaware of paths to citizenship." www.safepassageproject.org

U.S. Citizenship and Immigration Services (USCIS) maintains an excellent website for learning the most up-to-date immigration law. www.uscis.gov/archive/consideration-deferred-action-childhood-arrivals-daca

United We Dream seeks to "address the inequities and obstacles faced by immigrant youth." https://unitedwedream.org

Additional websites can be found in the chapter notes.

INDEX